DISCLAIMER

This is a work of fiction. Names, characters, places, events and incidents are either the product of the author's imagination or used in a fictitious manner.

Because the dog is the storyteller, the rules regarding proper grammar and punctuation are loosely followed.

Books by Jennifer Rae:
Kessen's Kronikles
The Adventures of a Cross Country Canine

Izzy Come…Izzy Go

Tansy's Tales

Brunch With Brightie
By
Jennifer Rae

DEDICATION

To the Dynamic Duo

They taught me the true meaning of unconditional love.
I am forever grateful.

Brightie

THE BRUNCH MENU

INTRODUCTION

Never in my wildest dreams did I ever believe that I might someday have a position of authority in my canine pack.

Shocking news...

Until two weeks ago, my dreams revolved around my being a princess or even a queen. Having the initials HRH, short for Her Royal Highness, stamped on all dog bowls and kennel mats placed throughout the entire house added to the splendor of the delightful dream. However, upon awakening from such an enjoyable dream state, I was faced with the reality of my situation. I was now the leader of the pack in my household that was quite affectionately called the sorority house. The name was chosen because so many female puppies came here for training, and male pups were always outnumbered.

Upon his retirement, our pack leader named Kessen unexpectedly designated me as his successor. I'm usually quite in tune with the comings and goings of the household, but I never anticipated anything close to that decision. Because our folks were puppy raisers for an assistance dog organization, year after year puppies passed through what seemed like revolving doors of the sorority house for training. As long as Kessen remained in charge, my position

3

as second in command of the canine pack remained stable. That position didn't bother me because leadership involved a lot of work, and I am opposed to all forms of exertion. Now, my elevation to the esteemed position of pack leader was totally contrary to my life's plan and not at all in keeping with my desire to live an effortless life.

Before I go any further, it would certainly help if I introduced myself. My given name is Brighton, but I'm usually called Brightie...unless I'm in trouble. When caught in some form of mischief, my given name is used in a most authoritative manner. While getting caught doesn't happen too often, when it does, consequences are administered in a swift and fair manner. Given my ability to learn from the results of misbehavior, I am called Brightie much more than Brighton.

I do enjoy a good time.

I'm a natural blonde and an extremely attractive mix of two different breeds of dogs: the Labrador Retriever and the Golden Retriever. Upon my arrival at the sorority house ten years ago, Kessen, the strong and confident leader of the pack, not only became my mentor but turned out to be my best friend as well.

Kessen was also recognized as the finest storyteller in the neighborhood. In fact, he initiated the tradition of storytelling time years ago when I was just a young puppy. Dogs from all over the neighborhood would gather to hear his stories that both thrilled and tickled their senses each and every time. The storytelling was held in the evening when

the light from the moon cast shadows through the trees...creating both an exciting and threatening setting. Kessen felt that type of setting encouraged the element of surprise and was a way of holding the full attention of his listeners.

He sure knew how to spin a yarn.

He was, indeed, the master of storytelling and spent the last few months passing that skill on to another member of our pack named Tansy. She was an enthusiastic puppy in training in our household, worked as an assistance dog for a few years, was retired when her partner's condition changed and finally came back to the sorority house to live. Tansy has been an asset to the household in numerous ways since she is devoted to the pack, respectful of others and picks up her toys as well as mine each evening before going to bed. Being chosen by Kessen to continue his great tradition of storytelling is by far her most notable contribution. Her picking up my toys is a close second in terms of being significant.

Was I slighted by Kessen's choice of having Tansy follow in his paw prints as resident storyteller? Not in the least. Learning the art of storytelling involves having good listening skills, attention to details and a flair for the dramatic. I certainly have those qualities but rarely use them...except for the flair for the dramatic. I specialize in that specific skill which is why I wasn't surprised when Tansy became the storyteller. I prefer my status as resident diva and pride myself in knowing that it's a recognized and unchallenged position.

However, some versions of stories as told by Kessen to Tansy, in my opinion, were somewhat influenced by either the elapsed time or the particular situation. As the new leader of the pack, I intend to share my own recollections of the events while exercising my own distinctive flair for the theatrical. I am not going

Tansy was the right choice.

to intrude in any way on Tansy's storytelling time since she spent so much time mastering that specific skill, and that interference wouldn't be fair to her. Instead, I will put my very own personal paw print on storytelling by not infringing on the evening time slot but by elevating the event to an even classier time frame...Brunch!

My storytelling is not going to rely on the moon and shadows from trees for an ominous setting. Instead, my event will take place mid-morning with the sun shining brightly on the deck. I believe this type of setting will not only dazzle those who attend but will also add a tone of sophistication to the event. As barks and howls of satisfaction fill the neighborhood, this event will soon be recognized as the embodiment of sophistication and will blossom into the ultimate in-spot for prominent canines. Too melodramatic? What can I say? I am, indeed, a diva but a delightful one if I might say so myself!

That being said, I hope you, the reader, will join me  as I share stories of my journey... beginning with my puppy days in California to my present-day rise to power as leader of the pack in the Midwest. Rather than follow a strict timeline of my life, I've chosen, at times, to deviate a bit by focusing on events and experiences for the sake of your total amusement. Perhaps these

The perfect brunch setting... stories might someday be thought of as entries from my diaries. With that possibility in mind, my imagination immediately envisions these personal recollections in print as the *Memoirs of a Delightful Diva*. Wouldn't that just be an awesome accomplishment as well as a splendid tribute to my life?

There I go again...lapsing into my flair for the dramatic. Sometimes, I just can't help myself. Nevertheless, I hope you enjoy reading my stories as much as I enjoy sharing them with you. As your hostess for this event, I invite you to join me as I begin...*Brunch with Brightie* .

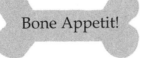

Bone Appetit!

THE JOURNEY

1

California Cutie

California, the place of my birth known as the Golden State, definitely lived up to its name. The sun shined gloriously on a daily basis giving the landscape a tinge of gold as the sky met the earth. Colorful rainbows frequently arched their way across the bluest of blue skies displaying nature at its best. Sad to say, I never really appreciated those

The California Cutie!

marvels of nature. After all, I was just a puppy and appreciation of my surroundings unfortunately wasn't a high priority. Rather than focus on the environment, my reality centered around eating, playing and sleeping as much as possible. Nevertheless, what I quickly learned was that one's idea of reality rapidly changed and not always in a fair way.

My name is Brighton, and I was the first born in a litter of six puppies. My litter was the result of mixing two special breeds of dogs…a Golden Retriever and a Labrador Retriever. According to my birth mother, my siblings and I favored the Labrador Retriever side in terms of appearance. I resembled my father, named Miller, more than any of the other pups in the litter. She said that Miller was the most handsome dog she had ever met, and my looking like him made me extra special. In her eyes, being the first born was supposedly proof of that fact. However, while being first is sometimes thought of as being the best or the winner, that premise just wasn't accurate in my situation. The issues of my birth order coupled with my petite size made a good case for being

My dad was so good-looking.

second or third. In spite of being first born, I was definitely not in the winning position in my litter. The other pups had some strange notion that my being first born somehow made me the leader of the pack...a position envied by the other members of the litter.

My other siblings were much larger, weighed more and as a result, got a lot more space at my birth mother's side during feeding time. While my mom told me that I was the light of her life, she had five other pups who brightened her life as well, and they had to be fed just as I did. Mealtime was a real scramble for suitable positions, and as far as I was concerned, size definitely mattered.

Without the benefit of sight in those early days, I had to maneuver through numerous obstacles just to get in position for feeding. My brother Bart became my champion and often moved other siblings out of the way so I might enjoy a meal. Little did I know that Bart was the first of many heroes who would enter my life and help me in difficult situations. As far as I was concerned, his being my first hero made him the most important one.

The weeks passed, and I, along with my siblings, greeted the world around us with eagerness and excitement. Nothing was too difficult or too challenging in this new setting. We were now eating regular puppy meals from a huge bowl under the supervision of our mother, had miraculously gained sight and were allowed unsupervised play in a small, grass-filled yard. What more could puppies ask for in terms of comfort?

Well, I had some reservations about all of that freedom. It was all well and good for most of the litter, but for me, that access to freedom was something I feared on a daily basis. Being so small as compared to my other siblings made me a perfect target for their competition for higher positions in the pack order. At first, I didn't care about who wanted to be first or second. I really didn't have any say in my birth order, but my siblings didn't see it that way. Each one wanted to be first, and ultimately, the pack leader. It really made no sense to me, but they were a determined group of puppies.

My simple goals of eating, playing and sleeping changed to include avoiding danger on a daily basis. At first, I was easily intimidated by this puppy power struggle. With the exception of Bart, my other siblings would confront me on a daily basis. Pushing, nudging and nipping became their game of choice, and I was the target. Bart would often come to my defense and shield me from their efforts to intimidate me. But, he couldn't be everywhere all day long, and I often found myself in vulnerable situations involving their game playing. Their taunts were not games to me.

I really didn't know what they expected of me, and what they hoped to accomplish with their actions. No matter what they did to me, I'd always be the first born, and nothing would ever change that fact. I attempted to explain to them that being born first didn't make me the pack leader. It just meant that I was born first…nothing more!

Since reasoning with them didn't work, I decided to  just hide from the group and find companionship with Bart whenever I could. We'd spend the day doing fun stuff like rolling around in the grass, eating grass and eventually spitting up grass. In our world, it was the trifecta of fun, and we gave each other silly nicknames during our shared play time. Because I was petite, blonde and

Bart was my handsome hero.

had long, curly eyelashes, Bart called me his California Cutie. Bart, looking nothing like me, was much larger in size, had a fluffy ebony coat and the darkest eyes I had ever seen. I called him my Handsome Hero. We knew they were silly names, but they were important to us.

Since all of the pups in the litter ate as a group, mealtime was a bit scary for me. Bart always led the way and made sure I wasn't bothered while eating. I learned to eat fast and then seek out the protection of my birth mother.

My mother was a kind, wise and loving mom. She noticed that my littermates intimidated me whenever they could and hoped that I would someday show my strength

Mom always knew how to help me.

and defend myself. Seeing that it wasn't happening, she decided to have *The Talk* with me. It wasn't about hiding or being pushed around, it was about reliance on my inner strength and using that power to prove to my littermates that I would no longer be intimidated just because I was the first born. My being petite didn't help because I was a bit of a munchkin compared to the others, but my mom insisted that inner strength didn't come in sizes. How did I get so lucky to have such a wise mother?

Well, let me tell you, I was now energized and determined to confront my littermates and show them that I was no longer their target. I told Bart about my intentions, and he was a bit doubtful that I could pull it off without some planning and a major growth spurt. But, I was determined to confront my littermates at the earliest possible moment before my enthusiasm dwindled.

15

I didn't have to wait long for that confrontation to take place. Just before breakfast the next day, I took some deep breaths, believed I was drawing on my inner strength and positioned myself in front of the food bowl. Bart thought that keeping them from their meal wasn't the best of choices, but he promised not to interfere even if I needed help. As my littermates approached, they chuckled as I faced off with them in front of the food bowl. I could tell that my inner strength was working because they hesitated. However, I was totally wrong in my assessment of that situation. They only hesitated in order to gain momentum to push me aside as if I were a fly bothering them in the yard. It didn't take much for them to send me flying because, as I mentioned a few times before, I was quite petite. In hindsight, Bart was correct about my needing more of a plan as well as my being able to pull it off on my own.

I was still determined as well as energized by my mother's encouragement. Since my chosen act of blocking their food bowl didn't work, I attempted a different approach...I'd act a bit weird. I wasn't even sure I could pull that off since it really wasn't in my nature to be assertive nor to act peculiar. Nevertheless, I'd have to try this tactic if I ever wanted to eat a meal in peace. Bart, listening to my plan, was still skeptical regarding the success of my plan, but once again, agreed to let me handle it myself.

As dinner time approached, I positioned myself in front of the food bowl as I had done earlier in the day. As they approached, I leaned forward on my front paws to steady myself and started to emit a low, raspy growl. It surprised me because I didn't even know I could make that type of sound. The strange noise momentarily stopped them, but as evidenced by my earlier attempt at breakfast, they believed that I was no threat to them. As I heard their chuckles, all of their taunts of the past weeks came welling up in my mind. Suddenly, something in me snapped. My low growl turned to a much louder version that even startled me. At that very moment, I lost total control of myself.

I curled my lips, growled, snapped and barked as I charged the group. Adrenaline surged through my body causing foam to gather on my lips giving me an even more threatening appearance. All of their daily intimidations flashed before my eyes as I ran toward them, and I was energized as they scattered in all directions with their tails tucked under them. I was a pup gone wild, and even Bart looked extremely concerned about my behavior and was tempted to run away.

Nevertheless, this totally unnatural behavior on my part worked. When my vision cleared and normal breathing returned, I saw that my littermates had found hiding places somewhere in the yard. The new knowledge that somehow my petite body was now a weapon of mass intimidation gave me a powerful feeling, and I knew that no pup was going to

No one bothered me now.

push me around ever again. My plan worked, but why didn't I feel better about it? In spite of their mean tactics,

17

seeing my brothers and sisters run away from me was very upsetting.

The days passed, and stories of my behavior as a demented puppy and bully spread to other litters in the area. No one pushed me around anymore, but no one except Bart wanted to be around me either. Sometimes I think he

I was such a lonely puppy.

didn't like me as much as he did before my crazed actions.

Now, I no longer trusted anyone because I was fearful that if I gave in and apologized, my littermates would start their mean games all over again. At meal time, I was allowed to eat first, and no one bothered me in the play yard. I should have been happy, but I wasn't. Something in me changed on that particular day. Parts of me that were considerate, loving and trusting were lost, and I'd never be the same, sweet pup who had the misfortune of being born first.

The weeks went by, and we were all getting ready to leave our mother's care and go off into the world. We were told that we had great adventures ahead of us, but we didn't know what that even meant. My mother understood what had happened on that fateful day that changed my life and

My adventure begins...

why my lack of trust would govern my behavior for a while. But, she believed that one day everything would change for me, and that sweet, petite puppy, who was the first born and light of her life, would learn to trust again. She was such a wise mother, and I hoped with all of my heart that she was right. Nevertheless, I didn't see that day coming any time soon…at least not for me.

The day came for us to leave the safety and security of our home and begin the next exciting chapter in our lives. We were going to families who would raise us for a year and prepare us for possible roles as assistance dogs to the disabled. To be honest, I didn't understand what they were talking about. However, as fate would have it, Bart and I were going to go on this great adventure together. This was such a wonderful surprise!

As several vans parked along the winding driveway, kennels were arranged inside the vehicles for transporting puppies to various parts of the country. I nestled closely to my mom one last time so I could hear her heart beat and thanked her for all the wonderful gifts she had given me. Her enduring love and heartfelt wisdom would remain in my heart forever. While leaving her saddened me, I was also excited to begin this next chapter in my young life. She reminded me of my inner strength and wanted me to know how very proud she was of me. Having heard her loving words gave me total confidence that I was ready for the adventures to come in my life. In my opinion, having that next chapter begin with my brother Bart was better than finding gristle on a soup bone. We were kennel-mates going off to see the world.

After settling into our shared kennel, we both took a long look through the van's back window at the only home we knew since we were born. As we left the driveway, our home gradually became smaller and smaller in size. When the van reached the highway, our home had totally disappeared from our view. Even though it was gone from our sight, that view was etched into our hearts forever. As Bart and I exchanged knowing glances, we were filled with excitement and looked forward to the adventures that were ahead of us. This California Cutie and her Handsome Hero were ready to take on the world one dog bone at a time. Little did we know what really awaited us when we finally reached our destination...

No disrespect intended, but since Kessen wasn't with me in California during my early puppy days, his versions of my beginnings in his stories were derived mainly from hearsay. Due to the unreliable nature of information passed from one canine to another over time, unintended discrepancies might have occurred. I'm not implying his versions don't have elements of truth in them...they most certainly do. However, my telling of the early California days is based entirely upon my experiences as they occurred and achieves total accuracy. Because Kessen was such a stickler for truth and accuracy, he'd thoroughly approve of this approach.

21

The Traveling Twosome

Bart and I were still brimming with excitement as the van traveled along the highway. The driver would occasionally check on us in his rear-view mirror to see if we were okay, but he didn't have to worry about us. We were having a good time watching the cars and trucks go zipping by. There were so many things to see as the van zigzagged through the traffic. Views of farms and fields turned into glimpses of homes, stores and big buildings. After a while, we came upon a huge, rust-colored bridge that seemed to have no end to it. Numerous cars traveled swiftly in each direction while people walked briskly along the sidewalks on each side of the traffic lanes. The wind was blowing fiercely as evidenced by the swaying of the van and people hanging on to their hats and scarves as they crossed the bridge. Looking below the bridge was an enormous expanse of blue water that seemed to have no beginning or end in either direction. This was such an incredible sight!

We had never seen or heard of anything like this before, and apart from this experience being so awesome, the view was also a bit frightening. I was so glad that Bart was sharing the kennel with me, and I think he was just as happy that I was there with him as well. Aside from the honking car horns and the van weaving around cars, there was just so much to see, and the bridge just seemed to go on forever. Was there an end to this enormous bridge and if so, what would we find on the other side? We finally reached the end of the bridge, and much to our surprise, we saw even bigger buildings at this end. These buildings seemed to touch the sky. I wished that we could have shared this experience with our mother. She really would have enjoyed either being with us on this trip or having us tell her about this awesome adventure. Little did we know that the trip was about to get even better.

The traffic increased as we left the bridge. In addition to cars and trucks, there were huge vehicles called busses that were used for transporting people. Our van driver was like a tour guide explaining things to us as we continued on our journey. We didn't understand most of what he was talking about, but the sound of his voice was reassuring. He told us that we were on a street called the Embarcadero that was heavily traveled by tourists on a daily basis. Shops dotted the right-hand side of the street, while on the left there was a waterfront area called Fisherman's Wharf. Numerous carts, having colorful canopies, were positioned up and down an extremely wide sidewalk bordering the dock. Each cart was filled with all varieties of seafood delicacies. The delicious aromas coming from the food carts on the wharf were making our mouths water. People were everywhere sampling the various foods on display in the carts. What an exciting way to eat!

On the other side of the wharf was a huge expanse of water where tour boats were moored and travel arrangements could be made. Strange, unfamiliar barking sounds came from unusual looking animals grouped together on floating rafts in the water around the wharf. Huge, low flying, squawking birds seemed to torment them with their fluttering wings. The van driver told us those honking animals were sea lions who lived in the waters by the wharf and were a major tourist attraction in the area. The low-flying birds, called sea gulls, lived in the area around the wharf and were constantly searching the waters hoping to find fish for their meals. Between the masses of people, the noise from the sea lions and the squawking birds, feelings of being overwhelmed were creeping into our bodies at a fast pace.

As we left the wharf area and continued along the Embarcadero, odd clanging sounds could be heard in the distance. Our van driver said those sounds were coming from the famous cable cars that transported people around the city. As one came by us, we saw this strange looking form of transportation, traveling on tracks and filled with people who really seemed to be enjoying the experience. As the bells clanged, the people cheered and applauded. So much was happening all around us that our minds were definitely on overload.

The traffic pattern seemed to change as the wharf disappeared in the distance, and sounds of the cable cars were no longer heard. Instead, loud roaring sounds seemed to come from the sky. Now what? If those sounds were coming from birds, they must be pretty big birds! Bart and I didn't know what to make of the situation. Our van driver attempted to enlightened us by saying we were nearing the airport, and as a special treat, we were going to fly across the country on a big bird in the sky. Honestly, we didn't understand a word he said. We just knew that some enormous birds were making loud noises above us, and we didn't know how to get away from them.

Suddenly, the van turned into a darkened garage, and only the van's headlights provided the light necessary

for traveling through the darkness. The van stopped suddenly when we reached a long ramp leading to a very wide doorway. Some people came out to greet us and were pulling a type of cart behind them with a strange looking kennel on it. It didn't look

This was a very strange kennel.

anything like our wire kennel. First of all, it was white and only the door was made of wire. The sides were solid except for small openings at the top. It didn't look like anything we had ever seen before. The van driver opened the back door of the van and gently transferred us, one at a time, to the strange looking kennel. He smiled at us and wished us well on our journey. We weren't sure what was going to happen next.

He then returned to his van and disappeared into the darkness of the garage. As van drove off, we felt the cart moving as our new kennel was pulled up the ramp and through the doorway. Bart was tall enough to look through the openings on the side, and I had to rely on looking through the wire door to see what was happening. People were walking all around us, dogs were barking in other kennels like ours, but we didn't recognize any of the dogs. Bart and I looked at each other and realized that all of the bravado experienced earlier about this new adventure was gone…really gone. We were two very frightened puppies, and our response was, in our opinion, very appropriate. Thinking that it would help, we both started to howl as loudly as we could. As our howling turned to screeching, the barking dogs in the other kennels joined in and barked even louder. There was total chaos in the room, and that frenzy only added to our fear.

Suddenly, a woman with a kind face appeared at our kennel door and talked to us in quiet, soothing tones that momentarily reassured us. As we slowly quieted down, the other barking dogs did as well. I guess one might say that we were the real instigators of the chaos, but we really didn't care about that. She told us that we were going for an airplane ride to an area of the country called the Midwest, and she would accompany us just to make sure we were safe. Once again, we didn't understand what she was saying, but her voice was calm and definitely comforting.

Bart and I were really tired from the traveling, the shuffling from the van to the airplane and especially from the howling and screeching. By the time the airplane left the runway and was high in the sky, its muffled rumblings served as a make-shift lullaby for our tired puppy bodies. While cuddled closely to each other, we quickly fell asleep.

Suddenly, we were awakened by some loud noises and were once again frightened. The woman with the soothing voice, seeing how frightened we were, came to our kennel and told us that nothing was wrong. The noise and rumblings were just from the plane's landing at the airport. Yet, another instance where we understood nothing but

When does the fun start?

were reassured by the sound of her voice. She then mentioned that in a few moments, we would meet our new families. New families? Now, that we understood! Weren't we going to stay together? Bart and I were family and needed each other. The thought that we wouldn't be together was too much to even consider after all we'd been through this day. The anxiety that overtook us earlier once again began creeping into our bodies, but there was nothing we could do.

As the plane bounced and rumbled to a stop, people shuffled around us, baggage was removed, and our kennel was taken from the plane and gently placed on a cart similar to the one that took us to the plane a few hours ago. We were then transported to something called a waiting room where some people were anxiously looking forward to our arrival. Suddenly, all of the events of the day seemed to take total control of my emotions. We said goodbye to our birth mother and the only home we knew. Then, we traveled in a van, on a cart, in

I really need to learn their language.

an airplane and on another cart. Now, we were meeting new families!

At times like this, I realized the importance of understanding just what people were saying. When and if things settled down, learning the language of humans was essential. I think Bart felt the same way as I did about that situation. For now, I'd just be myself and do what any puppy would do when overwhelmed...I began howling and screeching at the top of my lungs. Since I was positioned behind him in the kennel, Bart wasn't prepared for my unexpected outburst. He was momentarily shocked and frightened by my outrageous shrieking. Once he realized the disturbance was coming from me, he was able to relax a bit. We had to face facts...we were exhausted from the day's experience and had no control over our situation. Early this morning we thought we were going on a grand adventure.

So far, this day's events didn't come close to any of our expectations, and our being so very tired and stressed just added to the anxiety. From what we now heard, more surprises awaited us.

Families were waiting for us in a nearby room. Even though Bart attempted to calm me down, I continued to howl and screech. The people who were waiting seemed excited to meet us but looked somewhat stunned by the volume of my outbursts. I continued my frightening aria as the kennel door opened, and Bart was gently lifted from the enclosure. A kind looking woman held him in her arms and whispered soothing words to him. My shrieking continued as I realized that she was taking my brother away from me. Why was this happening to me...to us?

Suddenly, a kind-looking couple approached the kennel. The man, who was quite handsome, smiled at me while the woman, whose eyes seemed so gentle, lifted me from the airline carrier. She, too, held me close while gently rubbing my back. I do have to admit that having contact with people who obviously cared about me in spite of not even knowing me was such a comforting feeling...especially after the day Bart and I had. But, then I remembered that Bart wasn't going to be with me. Would I even get a chance to say goodbye?

Within minutes, I was reunited once again with Bart. We were then taken out to a grassy area by the airport and allowed to play a bit for the last time. We jumped around each other, rolled around the grass and cuddled together for the last time. Without having been told, we somehow knew we were going in different directions and would have different lives. Nevertheless, we'd always be family. Perhaps someday, we would meet again and reminiscence about our early days in California as well as the rigors of this nightmarish day that didn't show any signs of ending.

Bart reminded me that while I would always be the first born of the litter, that position had no significance in this new life. The problems I had with the other littermates that resulted in my change of demeanor were of no importance now. I was free to go back to being the sweet, kind puppy that he knew and loved. According to Bart, this family and change of homes were opportunities for new beginnings for me. Bart was such a wise puppy and a beloved brother.

I appreciated Bart's kind words of wisdom, but as far as I was concerned, the damage was done. Before I trusted anyone or anything again, that confidence would have to be earned. In the meantime, I'd keep my feelings to myself and remain aloof until I felt safe and secure once again. I didn't know how long that would take or if it would happen at all. I'd just have to wait and see.

After exchanging puppy nips and kisses, Bart and I hoped we'd find each other someday, and both of us promised never to forget how much we loved each other. He would always be my Handsome Hero. Even though we weren't in California anymore, Bart assured me that I would always be his California Cutie.

Settling into yet another form of transportation, I sat in the front seat of a car while the kind woman held me in her arms. I could feel her heart beating and was immediately reassured. Bart was in the front seat in another car and was being held closely as well. I will surely miss him just as he will miss me, but perhaps our lives will turn out for the best.

As our cars headed in different directions from the airport, I was already missing Bart. However, a small part of me was beginning to feel a bit better. Maybe it was the way I was being held by this kind woman or the way she gently rubbed my back that gave me hope for a new and better life. Every once in a while, the handsome man, who was driving the car, would reach over and gently rub my head and ears. While I didn't have the answers, I just knew their tender contact felt good.

Thoughts of the day tumbled through my mind as the car sped along the highway. Even though the traveling twosome were off to new and independent lives, one could only hope that the comfort of being held so lovingly signaled the bewildering events of this day were finally ending. I sincerely hoped that was true since this day was unquestionably one that I'd never forget...

Today was not a good day.

While Kessen heard of my intimidation by my siblings from other sources, he never really knew how important my brother Bart was to me during those difficult times. If Kessen had known what an important role Bart played in my life, he certainly would have mentioned him in his stories about my early puppy days. By including Bart in my stories and re-counting the significant role he played in my life, I'm honoring Bart in the only way I know how. Heroes, especially handsome ones, don't come along every day. Bart was my Handsome Hero, and I'm ever so fortunate to have him for a brother.

The New Digs

Leaving the airport and riding in another type of vehicle wasn't at all eventful due to the fact that I slept most of the way. The entire day of traveling was just too stressful for my puppy body. I thought I was tough but, apparently, not tough enough to withstand such a nerve-wracking day without collapsing from exhaustion. Too many changes in a short period of time, as well as missing my mother and my brother, made me consciously aware of my weaknesses.

I have to admit that I felt very safe being held by this nice woman after riding in various types of kennels, but I really didn't have too much of a choice in the matter. Kindness from others was not something I was used to in my original home. Sure, my birth mother and Bart were very kind to me, but those littermates of mine just didn't give up about my being first born and never let a day go by without finding ways to intimidate me. Maybe they thought it was just typical puppy play, but I was the target, and their actions didn't seem like fun to me.

I had to face the fact that my life in sunny California no longer existed. On the positive side, I no longer had to deal with the pressures of my littermates, but I now had to rely upon these strangers for everything. That fact, alone, was terribly frightening. I knew nothing about them, yet they seemed to like me before they really knew how difficult

I could be. Once I got a good night's sleep, my true behavior would surface. When that happens, these kind people might not think so highly of me.

The movement of the car's slowing down seemed to gently jog me from my nap. As I attempted to get my bearings, the car made a slow turn and pulled into a very long driveway. At the end of the driveway was a one level

What a great welcome!

house that didn't look anything like the house I came from this morning. This big house looked pleasant enough with its red brick exterior, white-framed windows surrounded by black shutters and contrasting gray-colored siding. But, what caught my eye was a concrete statue situated in a prominent place in the flower bed that surrounded the front of the house. The statue was an image of a dog, looking a bit like my mother, sitting upright while holding a basket filled with puppies. Was I lucky enough to be with a family who liked puppies? They must like them if they had a statue like that one in their flower garden. Was it an omen of good things to come? I wasn't sure, but I couldn't take my eyes off the statue as

They must be dog lovers.

the car came closer to the house. As we passed the statue and faced the front door, there were two other statues of dogs

36

positioned on either side of the front door. These dogs were sitting upright as well, but their baskets held bright, yellow flowers. This family must really like dogs, but would they like the real me and not just the tired pup barely moving in the front seat?

Once the car pulled into the garage, I was gently lifted from the front seat and placed on the concrete floor. The coolness of the floor was soothing on the pads of my paws as we made our way to the back door. I realized that in spite of my exhaustion, I was actually excited about this new place. Maybe it wouldn't be too bad, and let's face it, I didn't have much choice in the matter.

The nice couple opened the door and signaled for me to enter the room. Suddenly, I found myself facing four of

Who are you, and why are you sniffing me?

the tallest legs I had ever seen. As I looked up, I realized that I was standing in front of a rather large dog who had come to the door to greet me. He quickly moved backwards in order to get a good look at me and without any hesitation at all, began sniffing my body from every possible angle. While sniffing is an acceptable greeting among canines, I'd at least like to know his name before the sniffing began. Who was this giant dog anyway, and why was there a bit of a twinkle in his eyes? Somehow that twinkle meant something more than just a friendly greeting.

The handsome man told me that this dog was their very own dog named Kessen. While I lived with them, this dog was also going to be my new, big brother. What did he just say? A new big, brother? To my surprise, I understood what he said, and that was definitely not going to happen. I already had a brother who didn't look at all like this giant standing in front of me. As I looked up at the dog, I saw that when he heard he was going to be my big brother, which made me his little sister, that twinkle immediately disappeared from his eyes. He was just as surprised at our presumed relationship as I was. Perhaps having a little sister wasn't his idea of a good time either. At the very least, we had that in common. Upon hearing

You have got to be kidding.

that proposed sibling relationship, the big dog walked off and went to another room in the house. It didn't matter to me since I had no intentions of getting to know this presumed brother and a big one at that. What were these new people thinking?

Following that less than impressive meeting, the nice couple led me into their kitchen which would be my primary residence for a while. It was a huge room with a gate blocking entrance to the other part of the house. Located in the corner was an open-concept, wire kennel with a soft cushion inside, food and water bowls a short distance away as well as quite a nice selection of toys in a basket on the other side of the kennel. This couple obviously knew how to please a newcomer. I was already feeling better about the transition to the new digs.

After having a drink of water, I was taken outside to a huge yard. This area was nothing like the yard in my other house. Trees, shrubs and flowers surrounded the enormous

grassy area, and the flower beds had colorful bird feeders in the centers. The area was so colorful and a puppy's dream come true. I imagined running around the yard and feeling the coolness of the grass beneath the pads of my paws. I had a sudden burst of energy, but the collar and leash I

What a great yard! was wearing restrained me from running around the premises. Because I was small enough to fit through the fence rails, I wasn't allowed off my so-called tether. Nevertheless, I knew that with time, I would grow and eventually be allowed to run freely in the yard, and maybe there were other puppies in the area who would come and play with me. Those were all good thoughts until I remembered the giant dog, who was in the house, just waiting to greet me. What was his name again? It was a strange name, but he was also a strange dog. Some things just fit together.

By now, it was dark outside. After eating a very good meal, which surprisingly was exactly what I was eating at my other house, I was out to the yard one more time before going into my kennel for the night. I thought I was definitely ready for a good night's sleep, but sleep didn't come quickly. My mind started to relive the events of the day, and suddenly I was missing my mom, my brother and, surprisingly, even my other littermates. What was wrong with that element of my recollections? Anyway, loneliness set in, and my only response was that of a typical puppy…I began to howl. At first, it was a low-level howl but graduated to a high-pitched shriek. Even the giant dog came over to see what was happening.

The nice couple, realizing that it was my first night in a new home, began playing some soft music called canine lullabies that were meant to put lonely puppies to sleep. Were they serious to think that music would lessen the loneliness? My answer to that was to howl even louder, and the giant dog even moved a bit farther away in hopes of lessening the noise. Apparently, my true self was emerging, and this family was getting a taste of the quality of vocal tones contained in my petite body.

I'll admit it…I had no shame in terms of the howling. Sure, these people were good to me, and the giant dog even looked concerned for my welfare, but it didn't matter to me. I was lonely and about to pull out all of the stops while taking only a few short breaths between howls and shrieks. Looking a bit bewildered, the nice man covered my kennel with a sheet to either give me a bit of privacy or to avoid his own hearing loss. I wasn't sure what his motives were, but whatever they were, I wasn't about to stop.

My next move, in between screeches, was to pull portions of the sheet through the openings in the kennel. By doing that, I gained strength to resume howling. Once the nice man saw what I was doing, he removed the sheet, turned up the volume on the music meant to calm me and turned off the main lights. A small light, called a night light, was left on in hopes of lessening my fears. What happened next really surprised me…they just gave up. The nice man, the kind woman and the giant dog went to sleep leaving me with just a small light and my lonely thoughts. This was my first experience with recognizing the limitations of my power. Adjusting to these new digs would definitely take time, but I'd deal with that issue in the morning. My persistent howling led to my falling into a deep, well-deserved sleep…

Kessen's version of our first meeting was quite different from my recollection. It wasn't until months later that he told me how much he felt the need to protect me as part of being my big brother. He also told me that the volume of my howling at night was consistent with that of a feral beast, and no place in the house was safe from the sounds of my shrieking. I truly believe his assessments of my dulcet tones were quite harsh and totally unbelievable as far as I was concerned. That's all I'll say on the subject of my howling.

4

The Loud, Mean, Biting Machine

As morning came, I was startled out of my slightly groggy state by a pair of huge, brown eyes staring intently at me through the kennel wires. My first thought was to screech and howl, but once reality set in, I remembered this was the giant dog who greeted me last night…the one with

My nose will always be black!

the very long legs and quite a large pink nose. Who ever heard of a dog with a pink nose? My perfectly shaped nose was black as coal and would remain that color for the rest of my life. I was positive of that fact. Pink definitely did not fit into my sophisticated color palette, and I personally would not allow any changes to what I considered my self-proclaimed perfection.

The giant dog introduced himself to me once again, and I learned his name was Kessen. He came to this household from California a few years ago and was a puppy in training…just like my situation. He also apologized for his abrupt behavior the night before. Because he was so excited to meet me, his manners got lost in the shuffle. Since

43

I was so small, he didn't realize how frightening he must have looked. After seeing how distraught I was, he remembered what a difficult day it was for him when he left California to come to the Midwest. He also traveled on various types of transportation just to get here, but his arrival was during the winter. Snow filled the streets, sidewalks and yards, and no bit of green grass was seen in the yard. According to Kessen, remembering how strange it all felt for him during those first few days made him determined to help me in any way possible.

I felt a little bit better especially since he knew exactly what I had experienced the day before in terms of my getting here. He also understood the feelings of loneliness and loss that were all part of that horrendous day. I was almost liking him a lot until he mentioned how noisy I was during the night. He claimed that he could hear me all the way at the other end of the house, and the volume of my howling reached ear-shattering proportions. At first, he thought a wild animal had somehow gotten into the house. The screeching was this creature's way of seeking out prey, but then he remembered that I was the only one in the kennel. He just didn't think such blaring sounds could come from my tiny body without the use of a huge megaphone appropriately placed in my throat.

What's with that pink nose?

By this time, I was liking him a lot less and inquired about the color of his nose. It didn't exactly scream macho as far as I was concerned. He just laughed and informed me that it wasn't the color of the nose that made the dog, it was the dog having the nose. According to him, his colorful nose was the special nose belonging only to the leader of the pack, and it didn't get any more macho than that!

This so-called leader of the pack also had a black, nickel-shaped patch of fur on his side that distinguished him from the other dogs in his litter. He even boasted about having a tattoo in his ear. If he had that tattoo, I wanted to

He just might be macho after all!

see it in order to believe it. In the spirit of friendship, the giant dog leaned down and allowed me to look inside his ear. Judging by the size of his ear, I was expecting a pirate's hat or a coiled snake. Instead, all I saw was a tattoo that identified the year of his birth. Still, it was a tattoo and, in my mind, lent more credibility to his being macho.

Switching from thoughts of his appearance to his thoughts on leadership, I really wanted to laugh because he was quite serious about being the leader of the pack. What pack was he talking about, and where were the other members? Were they hiding in the house? As it turned out, the two of us were the only members of his so-called pack. The others would eventually come, but for now, he was the dog in charge...pink nose and all. Then, just to create some uncertainty in terms of my thoughts regarding self-proclaimed perfection, he told me that my nose would definitely change from black to pink as I grew older. That change in color was something I had no control over in terms of my appearance. It would definitely happen, and his only hope was that he be present when it did.

Who was he kidding? As far as his prediction of my nose turning pink was concerned, the likelihood of that happening was not even worth a moment's apprehension on my part. His attempt at kidding me was going nowhere since no one kids a kidder...especially one with a pink nose. Even though I didn't trust him, I was going to have some fun with this so-called leader of the pack. He had great potential for my amusement.

While it sounded like I knew what was involved with being a pack leader or even understood what that meant, I admit that I knew nothing about it. My littermates thought it was important in terms of status which was why they tormented me on a daily basis. But, did they really know what being the leader meant? I didn't have a clue about it, and perhaps they didn't either. I believed that Kessen, the giant dog with the huge pink nose and glaring eyes, had that information on his new agenda, and my learning curve was about to change.

After a nice meal and a romp in the yard while attached to a long tether, Kessen and I met for another attempt at a proper meet and greet. We faced each other, sniffed appropriately, and he began what would later be known as the first of many Puppy Training Seminars. The session included the household rules, appropriate puppy behavior and respect for authority.

My eyes glazed over as I pretended to listen to him but was shaken back to reality when he made mention of my mother and father. He informed me that the handsome man and kind woman of the household would be called my new mom and dad. Because they would care for me, make sure I was fed

What was he talking about?

and kept safe just as my real mother and father would if they were here, calling them mom and dad was appropriate.

Kessen went on to say that when he first came to the household, he had nicknames for them, but Sammy, the Golden Retriever who lived next door, explained how sensible it was to call them mom and dad. According to Kessen, it was just easier to give in and call them mom and dad before getting involved in the lecture series about parenting from the wise neighbor.

This new bit of information was totally puzzling. As much as I thought that Kessen might be giving me sound advice, my lack of trust re-emerged just as Kessen initiated some play time. As he bowed appropriately to engage in play, events of my being pushed, shoved and pulled by my littermates flashed through my mind. Without even thinking, I reverted to my bully behavior by growling, barking and lunging at Kessen…ending with a notorious nip with my razor-sharp puppy teeth. Taken totally by surprise due to my peculiar and otherwise rude behavior, he quickly

I was suddenly a bully again!

backed away from me while screeching in pain. For a moment, I thought he just might come rushing back to retaliate for my assault, and I was definitely no match for him in terms of body size and bite strength. What was my motivation for attacking such a large dog? As I watched him retreat, he gave me a look of disappointment and just left the room without even a backward glance. Then, I remembered Bart telling me that I could start fresh and leave that bully behavior behind when I came to the new place. Somehow, letting go of that behavior was easier said than done.

I was still out of control in my puppy frenzy when the new people came running to see what happened. They thought that perhaps Kessen had done something to frighten me. Seeing me spinning around in such an agitated state added to their startled looks. My frenzy continued as the gentle man picked me up from the floor. Holding me close to his body somehow helped to calm me down from the frenzy that had overtaken me. The folks just looked at each other, didn't know what started the ruckus and weren't sure what to do about it if it happened again. Though pint-sized, I was definitely going to be a challenge in the months to come.

Unfortunately, I wasn't anywhere near ready to trust these people, nor was I going to trust that giant dog who claimed be my big brother. I finally made a concession and began calling him by his name rather than giant dog. While I wouldn't admit it, calling him Kessen was a step in the right direction. Although he kept his distance from my lunges and sharp teeth, he seemed to take this big brother nonsense very seriously.

My strange behavior continued in a most inconsistent manner. When I wasn't trying to steal Kessen's toys, I spent the rest of the time air snapping, barking and howling at anything or anyone who came near me. The folks began my training and eventually resorted to wearing leather gloves when working with me.

I was a bit out of control.

Protecting their hands was a brilliant idea on their part considering I was nipping, lunging and biting them at every opportunity. Because of my behavior, I thought they just might send me back to my original home, but that never happened. They weren't giving up, and neither was I. Apparently, they had a great tolerance for pain!

A month later, I was taken for a car ride for some sort of surprise called a play date. I didn't know what that was, but since it involved play, I was thrilled. Kessen didn't come with us, and I'm sure he looked forward to the safety of the house without me in it. Even though I didn't know where we were going, I was excited and demonstrated that enthusiasm by screeching and howling...all the way to our destination.

As our car pulled into a driveway, I saw a black puppy sitting nicely in the grass with his owner. Surprise of all surprises, it was my brother Bart! Oh, my goodness! My heart leapt with joy and anticipation over seeing my brother once again. When the car door opened, I pushed and shoved against the kennel door in hopes of being released from my metal enclosure. However, the man, now known as my dad, held the door shut until I sat quietly. When he opened it again, if I lunged at the door, he'd shut it again. What was the point of opening it, if he didn't want me to come out? We did this a few times before I realized that if I sat quietly, he'd take me out. Duh! Perhaps I'm not the sharpest bone in the bag.

While it seemed like a waste of time, I complied by sitting, was finally taken out of the kennel and placed on the grass. I ran at top speed to greet my brother Bart. When we met, we jumped on each other and rolled around on the grass together. It was such a treat to see him once again. We both shared experiences for a while, played until we were exhausted and then were taken into the house where Bart lived.

We played a little bit more in the kitchen, but then something changed between us. Bart wondered if I were back to being my sweet self in my new home or if I had chosen to resume my intimidating behaviors in this new place. Intimidating behaviors? Did he think I enjoyed behaving badly with my littermates? He knew why I had to defend myself in my original home, yet I never really knew

My own brother was disappointed in me.

his thoughts about the way I resolved the issue. His disapproval was most evident, and at that moment, the fun ended. I no longer wanted to participate in this play date and made my feelings evident by chasing Bart around the room to make him take back his unkind words. I had him cornered under a kitchen chair, but before he could respond to my demand, I was suddenly whisked away by my dad's strong but gentle hands. Evidently, the scheduled play date was definitely over. Faster than a flea jumping on a dog, I was back in my kennel in the car. While on the way home, I kept hearing my brother's words over and over again in my mind. Having him disappointed in me was just another reason to resume howling. While I wasn't really feeling like howling, I did it anyway.

As a means of encouraging socialization, the folks enrolled me in something called Puppy Kindergarten. It was a class meant to instill proper behavior between other dogs as well as some pretty basic obedience commands. I already knew my name, how to sit and do some other things, so I spent time observing the other pups in action. Because my classmates seemed very nice, I was momentarily tempted to be appropriate in terms of behavior but gave that up quickly when one of the class members unexpectedly lunged at me. I returned the gesture a lot faster than that pup anticipated and was never bothered by him again. I eventually played nicely with the group but remained vigilant for any signs of intimidation.

I also attended special classes for groups of dogs who were in the same type of training as I was. We were all potential assistance dogs for the disabled. I still didn't know what that was, but all of the pups were about the same age, and it was fun playing with them for a while. None of them seemed at all threatening, so I behaved myself most of the time. However, when it came time for the group leader to demonstrate nail clipping, I wanted no part of that situation. Slinking back towards a corner to avoid being chosen for the demo was definitely a mistake. Doing that maneuver drew attention to my lack of interest in participating and made me a perfect candidate for the endeavor.

Nobody touches my nails!

I made it very clear that I was very particular about my appearance. My nails were my business, and no one was going to touch them much less cut them. Once again, I did not anticipate the determination nor the strength of the group leader. In spite of my wrestling and twisting, I finally gave in and allowed the nails on my front paw to be clipped. Surprisingly, it didn't hurt at all and was, in fact, a form of pampering that I had never experienced before. After that first paw was done, I was glad I had three other paws. However, I didn't want the group leader to believe she had won the nail-clipping challenge, so I struggled just a bit as she held each paw. I know that was very immature, but I was a puppy and expected to act accordingly. I was only living up to expectations and age appropriate behavior.

That afternoon, I also realized that I had a lot to learn and needed to be open to more experiences instead of constantly keeping my guard up for signs of intimidation by others. Was I beginning to trust others? Seemed much too soon for that change in attitude.

On the way home, while howling at the top of my lungs, I thought about everything I had learned that afternoon. While I didn't know it at the time, I was in for another learning experience, and it wasn't going to be pleasant. That morning, the folks had changed my regular car kennel for a canvas traveling crate. The wire walls were replaced by a type of netting that was flexible allowing me to rest on the walls comfortably. On the way to the group class, I howled, barked and screeched without any terrible occurrence. The folks ignored my atrocious behavior and, in my mind, were really into pain. However, on the way home, I didn't realize how very close my mouth was to the netting of the crate. During one of my more enthusiastic barks, I got too close to the kennel wall, and my mouth got stuck in the webbing. If the folks thought my howling was intense before getting my mouth stuck, they were now in for a great surprise. Startled by my screeching and sensing it was more than just the usual disturbance, the folks stopped the car and began the task of extricating my teeth from the webbing. Because I was frightened, my teeth gripped the mesh even tighter so calming me down was the first challenge. Eventually, as the folks gently stroked my back and spoke softly to me, I relaxed my grip on the mesh. That enabled them to free my teeth from the netting of the kennel wall. Needless to say, we were all exhausted from the

experience. Never let it be said that I'm not a speedy learner...this pup never screeched in that scary canvas crate again!

When we got home, I told Kessen about my

I learned an important lesson today.

stressful experience. He thought it was quite funny since he had been listening to my howling and shrieking for weeks. He also had been my own personal pin cushion since I grabbed onto his face at every opportunity knowing that he wouldn't dare retaliate against his little sister. Let's face it... I had it made. However, my fun was about to end. Kessen then told me that because I continued with this odd form of misbehavior, the folks were forced to bring in the Big Gun. I, personally, thought Kessen was just trying to frighten me, but two days later when the doorbell rang, and Kessen ran to a particular throw rug on the floor, I knew I was in for some trouble. Kessen, the leader of the pack, was assuming a submissive stance on that rug. For the leader of the pack to do that meant trouble. Perhaps the Big Gun was real, and I was in for a rude awakening. Looking for assurance from Kessen, all I saw was the look of satisfaction on his face. The opening of that front door signified the ending of his days of being my own personal pin cushion. The loud, mean, biting machine was in for a very new experience...

I really owed Kessen an apology for my inappropriate behavior during my first weeks at the new place. He took his job of big brother very seriously, and I just ignored his sincerity. Seeing his look of satisfaction regarding the arrival of the Big Gun should have been an adequate warning that I had gone a few paw steps too far...not just with him but with the folks as well. As I said before, I was a puppy and just living up to puppy behavior expectations. Who was I kidding? I was way over the line and had a rude awakening in my future. How did I know? Kessen smiled!

5

Return of the Big Gun

Was Kessen simply attempting to frighten me into submission with his talk about the Big Gun or just pulling my paw? What kind of name was the Big Gun anyway? When the doorbell rang, and Kessen assumed a submissive position on a specified throw rug in the foyer, I had a hunch he might be serious. After all, he was the declared leader of the pack, so why would he assume a humble position? Either the Big Gun was the chief dog of the doghouse, or Kessen was just pulling a fast one on me. I wasn't sure what was going on until the door opened.

This dog meant business.

It was as if a halo of sunlight surrounded this guest as he entered the foyer of the house. His arrival, missing only the sound of trumpets, was awesome in its dramatic effect. A silken-haired Golden Retriever, widely known in canine society as the Big Gun, surveyed the household situation with only a slight nod of his head and a steely gaze. With a wave of his majestic tail, this was a dog who knew exactly what needed to be done. In spite of my youth, I sensed the possibility of trouble in the discipline department.

Now, I thought Kessen was a giant, but this dog was at least a head taller in size. Noticing Kessen in such a submissive stance was enough for the Big Gun to give him a slight nod of approval. Kessen beamed with appreciation at the recognition sent his way. It was obvious that the Big Gun was a force to be recognized

The Big Gun nodded his approval.

especially in his presence. At least, that was what Kessen believed. I, on the other paw, had different thoughts about this distinctive guest in the house.

Once I got over the effects of his grandiose entrance and Kessens's obvious awe of this stately dog, I realized that he was just another dog to contend with in my quest for behavioral independence. After all, the Big Gun had equipment just like every other dog...a head, a body, four legs having paws and a tail. Although I had to admit that his angular head undeniably represented his breed in a most regal manner. His body was well-toned for a dog his size, and his paws and nails were perfectly manicured. The motion of his stunning, feathered tail as it swished from side to side actually created a slight breeze. Perhaps this dog was really a force to be reckoned with while visiting the house, but only time would tell. Even as a young puppy, I had a couple of unique moves of my own, and I was not afraid to use them.

While totally ignoring me, the Big Gun walked through the house, and Kessen followed in yet another dutiful fashion...behind him. Since when did Kessen walk behind another dog? Minute by minute, this situation was bordering on the bizarre. I was thoroughly puzzled by the events, but my confusion was short-lived.

Faster than the blink of an eye, I found myself face to face with the Big Gun. How did he move so quickly, and why didn't I notice? He was even bigger in size as he lowered his head to meet mine and stared directly into my eyes. Because I believed his steely gaze was capable of boring a hole into my head, I quickly looked away

This dog was serious!

to avoid any cranial injury from those uncanny eyes. Yet, when I did that, he suddenly smiled. While I didn't realize it at the time, I had inadvertently shown respect to him by looking away. If I couldn't look at him, how would I know what he wanted me to do?

This encounter with Linus was all too baffling, and Kessen wasn't about to offer any assistance either. He just sat on the other side of the room with a goofy look on his face. I was definitely going to pay for using his face as a pin cushion these past few weeks. This situation must be the *karma* catching up with me that Kessen talked about every time I lunged or nipped his face. I never knew what he was talking about…until now.

I had to take a moment to figure out what my next move would be. Regaining my bravado was first and foremost on the list. I finally got the courage to look back at the Big Gun, and surprisingly, his eyes had tempered in their gaze. He told me his name was Linus and was invited to the house for puppy socialization purposes. I was the puppy, and he was the socializer. He was called the Big Gun because he was the last resort in the tool box of socialization techniques used by both humans and canines. His job was to encourage attitude adjustments in unruly pups when the traditional training techniques fell outside typical capabilities. In other words, I was in desperate need of some puppy etiquette, and he was here to see that I learned the

Linus wasn't fooling around.

basics. Linus also mentioned that his techniques were not standard, but *always*, and he emphasized the word *always*, were effective. Leaving the sorority house without the successful socialization of a pup was not an option as far as he was concerned, and I was to take special note of that fact. His tempered gaze was gone as he made it perfectly clear that he was here to stay until my inappropriate, silly behavior changed. At that moment, I believed his eyes actually glowed…resembling a weird alien creature of the night.

At first glance, this situation did not look good for me, but I decided to call upon my inner strength and demonstrate my independent nature. Showing fear was not an option, and the first significant move was to call him by his name rather than rely on his reputation as a weapon of socialization. In my mind, that decision made him more of a regular dog and less of a monumental threat to my carefree existence. In hindsight, I should have had a better plan.

Linus just stared at me with those chilling eyes and waited for my next move. He looked briefly at Kessen, who was still smiling like a dog who had found the marrow in a soup bone. Without any warning whatsoever, Linus' steely eyes were staring in my face once again. I'll admit, I was intimidated and backed away slowly. Apparently, my response was fitting since a bit of a smile or perhaps a smirk appeared on his face. While I wasn't entirely certain, I assumed he was just getting started.

Now, we were going out to the yard for some rules of behavior. Really? I needed another lecture like I needed fleas! But, Linus led the parade to the yard as Kessen pushed me aside to get into his position behind Linus, and I was last in this so-called parade. The first lesson was apparently learned. I was supposed to position myself behind Kessen wherever we went. What a Male Dogs' Club this was turning out to be, but I was outnumbered due to my femininity, size, weight and lack of seniority. I'm young but certainly not stupid. My only option was to go along with the program.

Linus took the time to explain his process of a Three Step Action Plan. Knowing what to expect when I made behavioral choices, I would already know the consequences of my behavior. That seemed fair to me at the time. If and when I attempted to lunge, bite, snap or growl at him or at Kessen, he would first snarl his lip as a warning. That tactic didn't seem like much of a threat to me, but it was, after all, just meant as a warning. If I continued, he would add a low growl to the process. Now, that seemed more like some action to me, but I've been growled at before, didn't back away and wasn't about to start now. The final step in Linus' plan was a muffled snap...not meant to harm, but to warn of the possibility.

Who was he kidding? That Three Step Action Plan was supposed to deter me from lunging at Kessen, eating from the food bowl first or stealing toys from him? I wasn't very old, but I wasn't born yesterday. That plan was ridiculous, destined to fail, and Linus was just wasting his time. While Linus referred to his plan as teaching puppy etiquette, I called it downright nonsense. As I looked around the yard, I saw Kessen nestled comfortably under the shade of the maple tree. I should have known from his expression that I misjudged the entire situation.

Well, let me say that my bravado was short lived in the sense that I never anticipated the visual impact of the curled lip when it was meant to warn, the low growl that chilled my bones, and the muffled snap that almost took my eyes out the first time I attempted to take a toy away from Linus. Because he was so close to biting me, my eyes got cloudy from his breath. That's how close he was to me and how easily he might have removed my eyes and nose if he were so inclined. This dog was serious about his job and demonstrated his dedication to a productive work ethic...in his very first attempt.

Now, I really had to re-think my behavioral activities and quickly moved to a secluded part of the yard. As I glanced at Kessen, he was rolling around in the grass and laughing. It must have been that *karma* thing again, and he was enjoying every minute of it. I didn't think it was very appropriate for the pack leader to respond in that manner, but realized that while Linus was here, Kessen was no longer in charge. He was free to behave in any way he chose and was taking full advantage of the freedom.

As dinner time approached, I ran to the house before either of the members of the Male Dogs' Club ventured toward the house. While Linus and Kessen approached, I circled the food bowls and deliberately taunted them. Since they were both glaring at me, I assumed those annoyed looks were probably just meant to frighten me. Kessen, living up to his standards as my older brother, wasn't about to retaliate, and Linus was a guest in the house and not likely to bite members of the household. That was my foolish mindset as I continued to circle the food bowl.

Might I add, I was pushing my luck, and Kessen's warning glance made me hesitate for just an instant. In that moment of uncertainty, Linus made his move. Like a stealth bomber, he was silently and swiftly in my face with that steely glare of his eyes forcing me to back away from the food bowls. He was obviously multi-tasking since he had both a quivering lip along with a low growl very close to my face. This dog was definitely a serious threat to my well-being, but before he got to the muffled snap, I was out of striking range of his teeth and quickly out of the room. I wasn't the sharpest treat in the treat bag, but my agility made up for the lack of mental awareness. Because my young bones were flexible, I was capable of rapid, backward scooting. That skill really came in handy in this particular situation and probably saved the condition of face.

For the next few days, I continued to taunt Linus, but the teasing gradually decreased. Linus wasn't giving up, and his teeth were getting closer and closer to my nose.

Taunting Linus was risky business!

Kessen warned me that as long as I persisted and refused changes in my behavior, I was going to be plagued by Linus at every turn. Linus was going to stick to his plan, and he was much older, wiser and had a full set of big-dog teeth.

Having Linus lose patience with me wasn't going to end well.

While in the yard, I had time to dwell on the events of the past few days. If truth be told, the presence of Linus, his Three Step Action Plan as well as his objectives for teaching unruly puppies was well-intended. I wasn't always behaviorally challenged and a bully. I used to be a sweet puppy before I had to defend myself from my siblings. However, maybe I didn't have to act that way anymore. I had to face the fact that Linus wasn't going to give up until I demonstrated appropriate behavior. Kessen deserved respect not only as the pack leader, but as my older brother as well. These thoughts filled my mind and robbed me of the comfortable nap I was so used to having while in the yard.

As it turned out, each passing day brought me closer and closer to Linus...not as an adversary, but as a friend. When I wasn't taunting him, and he wasn't snarling and growling at me, we actually bonded in a strange way. I was trusting that he wanted what was best for me.

I don't remember the actual moment I felt the change in my disposition, but I suddenly felt better about myself. Kessen knew my behavior was changing from unruly to compliant and trusting once again. Allowing Kessen to go to the food bowl first, not stealing his toys and just falling in line behind him when going outside to the yard were already natural behaviors for me. I never even thought about lunging or biting him either. I felt good about the changes I made in my conduct and actually liked the puppy I had become.

Linus sure was a great influence on me, and his pride

Linus was a cool dude!

in my behavioral changes was a great help to my self-esteem. I wasn't fearful of his Three Step Action Plan anymore because he didn't need to use it. I now relied on his words of wisdom rather than the fear of his teeth threatening the perfection of my face. I thought of him as my friend now and was sad because he would soon be leaving us for another gig with an unruly pup.

While Linus often turned his head if someone wanted to take a photograph of him, he actually allowed a *selfie* for me. What an awesome moment that was!

Much to Kessen's delight, Linus' job in this house was finished. It was another success story for him...another notch on his collar for a job well done. As a side note, Linus had more notches on his collar than I had teeth! The Big Gun came, conquered and had now left the building.

I learned a lot from Linus.

I'll never forget the week that Linus spent with us. It was full of many surprises, and the greatest surprise of all was my learning to trust again and be the pup I had been during my early days in California. My mother and Bart would be pleased with the changes in me. Thanks to the return of the Big Gun to this house, I learned how to behave with the canines of the world. Now, I had to work on my trust issues with the folks. I wasn't there yet, but with Linus' teachings, Kessen's guidance and my perseverance, anything was possible...

Kessen's version of my interaction with Linus was a much kinder version than I recalled. From his point of view, I actually learned a lot faster than he did when Linus came to visit him. In fact, Kessen reported that when Linus came to the house to correct his behavior, he actually thought Linus was coming for a slumber party and jumped all over Linus when he entered the house. I would have given up treats for a week just to have witnessed that scene. Now, that was karma at its best!

6

Slipping and Sliding

In the days following Linus' visit, I continued to behave properly toward Kessen, but as the days turned into

Mischief was my new name.

weeks, Linus' energy slipped away along with my resolve to behave appropriately. I gradually found myself rushing up to the food bowl, staring enviously at Kessen's toys and not really allowing him priority entrance into the yard. The element of real danger in doing those behaviors was thrilling in a strange sort of way. Would Kessen retaliate when my paws really crossed the line, or would he continue to protect me as required in his role as my big brother?

While I felt better about myself when I did things correctly, being good all of the time was exhausting and lacked pizazz. In fact, it was downright boring for a young puppy who thrived on excitement. What I needed was a balance of good and bad behavior to keep me on the road to happiness. It turned out that my chosen road was the one less traveled...at least in this household.

Kessen ignored my transgressions for a few days but tossed aside his commitment to big brother protection when I crossed the line and, might I add, crossed it bigtime. It turned out that Kessen had a very special toy...a nasty, blue. saliva-tinged ring toy. He would often take it into the yard, run around the perimeter once with it in his mouth and then settle down under the maple tree with the toy between his front paws. Because of its revolting condition, I never thought about stealing it from Kessen much less playing with it. There were other toys in his toy box that were much cleaner and guaranteed more fun, but on that particular day, his disgusting, smelly ring toy beckoned to me like bacon-flavored jerky left on the kitchen counter. My resolve to be good went right down the drain of common puppy-sense, and I didn't care one bit about the risks involved.

Did I secretly have a death wish?

Nevertheless, I needed a well-thought-out plan in order for my scheme to be successful. Running up to him and grabbing the toy from between his paws was a suicide mission. That ring toy was immensely special to him and having me steal it was going to release the demon in him... if he had one. Up until now, I hadn't seen any signs of demonic behavior in him, but those strong, silent ones were the type to watch out for when on the road to misbehavior.

What I needed was a distraction...a well-planned event that would take his eyes off his beloved toy. Yet, I never saw anything capable of doing that, but I wasn't about to give up. With each passing day, that ring toy became more and more of a trophy worth the danger. Then, in spite of my waiting for the right moment, the opportunity arose without any preparation whatsoever on my part. Our neighbors had a backyard barbecue planned for friends. As their guests arrived, one particular guest was the perfect distraction I needed. Sporting a rhinestone-studded collar, this gorgeous, female Standard Poodle pranced into the neighboring yard from the house next door. Her well-manicured nails, painted a vivid red, provided a stark contrast to her snow-white, impeccably groomed coat as she surveyed the premises. As she moved her head from side to side, all she needed was a crown to qualify her as a princess.

I'll admit that for a moment, I was mesmerized by her majestic appearance. Being extremely particular about my own appearance was, in my opinion, my most endearing quality, and seeing this visitor as perfection on four paws was breathtaking. Although Kessen thought of my considered perfection in appearance to be superficial, I believed he was envious of my success in reaching the height of femininity. He, on the other paw, was just the leader of the pack and, might I add, had a pink nose. How masculine was that?

I had to snap out of my admiration of this visitor and focus on the theft. To minimize my high esteem of her, I dubbed her the Princess Pooch. That name made her less of the epitome of perfection in my so-called superficial mind and more of the distraction I needed for success in my endeavor. Seeing Kessen looking so favorably at the grand female in the next yard provided my one and only opportunity to grab that ring toy. I just needed a slight advantage, and the Princess Pooch provided the time I needed...or so I thought.

Approaching Kessen from behind as he moved toward the Princess Pooch gave me the best access to his toy. With that advantage in mind, I quietly rushed across the grass at full speed. I was within seconds of reaching the toy when Kessen spun around and faced me applying all three elements of Linus' Three Step Action Plan at the same time. I mistakenly thought Linus was the only dog who used that technique. If I had known Kessen might use that tactic with me, my plan might have been different...too late now. Suddenly, I was faced with a curled lip, a low growl and a less than muffled snap that showed his huge teeth coming toward my face. Attempting to stop quickly caused me to slide almost into his teeth. This challenge wasn't the same as taunting him by the food bowl or running out to the yard in front of him...this scheme of mine was a personal affront to him. Seeing his enormous teeth up close made me realize that I had made a huge mistake. This wasn't the big brother facing off with me. Instead, it was the leader of the pack proving his superiority, and he wasn't smiling through those gigantic teeth.

What I didn't understand was how he saw me coming towards his toy. I was fast, quiet and using the Princess Pooch as the ultimate distraction. In terms of diversions, she was my guaranteed treat in the food bowl.

At this stressful moment, my only conclusion was that Kessen had eyes in the back of his head, and I should have prepared for that possibility. As far as I was concerned, it really didn't matter how he saw me coming. What mattered most was the consequence for my thwarted attempt at personal theft.

What saved me was his reliance on always acting appropriately. He wasn't about to punish me with the Princess Pooch watching the spectacle from the next yard. Maintaining decorum as the leader of the pack while she looked on was his only choice at the moment, and he couldn't let personal feelings enter into his dealings with me as she watched. I could tell that she was impressed with his restraint, but I saw the threatening look in Kessen's eyes as

How would Kessen punish me?

he gave me a backward glance, moved towards her and left me all alone in the big yard. I was definitely going to pay the price for my reckless endeavor, and in his own unique style, he made me wait for the consequence. Waiting was far worse than any immediate punishment I might have received.

After the Princess Pooch left the premises, I waited and waited for Kessen to approach me with my punishment. The numerous possibilities for penalties swirled around in my head as he avoided any and all contact with me. I guessed that he wanted to cool down before he disciplined me, but once again, I was very wrong. Punishment, in any form, wasn't coming my way in the near future. Instead, I was faced with not knowing what would happen or when any penalty would be administered. Yet, his disappointment in me was probably worse than any punishment that he might have given.

That day, I realized the difference between the road less traveled, which involved a combination of good and bad behavior, and the road to happiness...that of good

I was not very nice today.

behavior and pride in one's good works. Having Kessen disappointed in me was far worse than I had ever imagined. I never thought stealing his toy was such a big deal. But, it wasn't my silly attempt at blatant stealing that disappointed him...it was the stealing of his special toy, a toy that meant so much to him, that really disappointed him.

I learned a huge lesson because of what happened that day. In the future, I might unintentionally slip into some inappropriate behaviors...slide backwards in my progress toward good behavior or move, unexpectedly, away from the behaviors that made me feel genuinely good about myself. Nevertheless, I would try to not let that happen, and the words *slipping and sliding* became my reminder in the years to come of the cost of choices in terms of conduct. In doing that, I would hope not to slip or slide into inappropriate behaviors, and Kessen would never be disappointed in me again...

While Kessen never told me why his ring toy was so special, Sammy, our wise neighbor, told me the history behind the ring toy. Kessen received that toy from his sister, Kelyn, before they were separated years ago, and that toy was the only connection left to his family. Although that explained his love for that nasty, smelly ring toy, his love of the family's connection made my decision to steal that toy so much more terrible than I thought at the time. Shame on me.

Risky Business

For days following the Ring Toy Caper, Kessen made no effort to be anywhere near me. I felt his disappointment every time I walked into a room when he'd get up and leave

I spent a lot of time alone.

as I entered. Without knowing how to make it up to him, I found myself having a lot of alone-time. The folks noticed the change in both of our behaviors toward each other but didn't have a clue as to why it occurred. They were very disappointed that we weren't co-existing in a typical friendly manner, but the positive spin on that situation was lack of chaos in the house. Without the sounds of jaw sparring and air snapping that were typical of our prior interactions, the house was lacking in any sort of noise. Although the silence was a bit eerie for a house having an adult dog and a puppy learning to co-exist, the peacefulness was a welcomed change for a while.

Because I spent a lot of time by myself, I came up with a plan that just might get me back into Kessen's good graces. If I followed the teachings of Linus and didn't deviate in any way from good behavior, Kessen just might relent and spend time with me again. Since I couldn't run that plan by him, I just decided to put it into action.

That day, I waited for him to eat his meal first before I came anywhere near the food bowl. That was a challenge for me because I was always hungry and would eat dust if I could find any bits on the floor. As I passed him on the way to the food bowl, he didn't even cast a glance my way. I was a bit disappointed, but it was just the first attempt to win back his friendship. Rather than just ignore his toys, I brought one of my most valuable toys to his toy box. Giving my special shoe toy to Kessen was, in my mind, a huge attempt at apologizing. What sensible dog wouldn't cherish that

How can a dog resist a shoe?

toy? That shoe toy meant the world to me, but I hoped the act of giving it to Kessen would contribute more towards reconciliation. However, Kessen didn't even look at it. I was really at a loss now as to what to do next. What else was there to do?

As I said those words to myself, the solution came to me...I had to make friends with the folks. That would make Kessen happy. Until now, each day of training was a battle with them, and the routine was the same. They would each put on leather gloves as they entered the kitchen, otherwise known as the battleground, and I'd run at them full speed, grab onto some part of their bodies or lunge unexpectedly at any unprotected area. Because they believed in reinforcing positive behavior and ignoring the negative, I wasn't punished in any way for my aggressive issues...although they did wear leather gloves. Anyway, I'd be good for a while and get rewarded but would eventually go back to my lunging and grabbing. It was, in fact, a cycle of stupidity. The fact that I thrived on food and got treats when I was good, behaving otherwise was so very foolish on my part. However, it didn't stop me from misbehaving in that manner. I knew the folks were worried about my inconsistent and somewhat aggressive behavior. While the organization for assistance dogs was willing to take me back, the folks weren't ready to give up on me. That fact just proved they thrived on pain and punishment!

What was wrong with me?

Because I had so much time to think about my behavior, I believed it all came down to trusting them. But, why didn't I trust them? They were kind to me, kept me safe, fed me on a regular basis and put up with my antics. I even began calling them mom and dad a few weeks earlier. Why was it such risky business to trust them? If I had the answer to that question, I'd know how to get back into Kessen's good graces. There just had to be a way for me to take that risk and let go of the mistrust that seemed to govern my behavior with them. Stopping my lunging and biting while doing daily tasks wasn't significant enough. Whatever I chose as the right thing to do had to involve a greater risk on my part. The folks were already taking risks by continuing to work with me. I needed to change my thinking with regard to them. Linus helped me change my behavior with Kessen, so I knew I was capable of changing my behavior. I just needed the right event to let go of the mistrust I felt towards the folks. Why did letting go seem like such risky business to me? It just didn't make sense.

I didn't have to wait long for the right opportunity to arise for letting go of my trust issues. The occasion was doubly significant because it occurred in the kitchen area that was considered the battleground for my antics. Since I was slated as a potential assistance dog, my training included moving in and out of various forms of kennels. I already enjoyed the solitude of my open-concept, wire kennel and went in and out on command. The canvas traveling crate had its dangers with the mesh walls, but getting my teeth stuck in that webbing once was enough for me to treat that enclosure with the utmost respect. Now, the folks brought a new type of kennel onto the battleground for a new experience. It was very similar to the one I shared with my brother Bart on the airplane. The sides were mostly solid with small openings at the top and had a wire door on the front. Somehow, seeing that type of kennel was, at first, a bit intimidating.

Mom sat down on the floor next to it and called me to her side. She was proving to be quite a risk taker considering the fact that she wasn't even wearing those leather gloves. Of course, I was losing some of my baby teeth so it wasn't quite as risky as it might have been two weeks earlier when I had a mouth full of razor sharp, puppy teeth. However, I still had enough teeth in my mouth to inflict some pain if I chose to do so. Anyway, she opened the wire door, looked directly at me while holding a treat in her hand and gave me the command to enter. Even though I knew that command, I wasn't quite sure that I wanted to go into that enclosure...even with the enticement of a treat. Seeing me hesitate, my mom moved closer to the kennel and was almost level with my face. Dad, seeing this move on her part, warned her about being so close to my face because of my tendency to lunge unexpectedly. Mom didn't flinch at his words and mentioned that she trusted me to do the right thing. She trusted me? I never gave her any reason to feel that way in the past, so why would she take such a risk now?

I was quite puzzled by her behavior but went into the kennel anyway, turned around to face the front of the kennel and assumed a sitting position. I just sat there for a few moments while trying to figure out why my mom was such a risk taker and trusted that I wouldn't lunge at her as I had done many times before this event.

Sitting there, I realized this was my opportunity to make things right with Kessen and let go of my feelings of mistrust with the folks. It was risky but definitely worth the attempt. When Mom gave the release command for me to exit the kennel, I hesitated but then slowly walked out of the kennel. However, I wasn't finished yet because I had one more step to take...one that would free me of my trust issues. Rather than run off into the kitchen or lunge at either my mom or dad, I chose to gently climb onto her lap and settle into a nice, comfortable position. The folks were stunned into silence, and Kessen, watching from the other side of the room, brushed his face with his paws because he wasn't sure what he had witnessed.

For me, it was the moment that I decided to end the cycle of mistrust that governed my life since my puppy days in California. As I looked up from my comfortable position in my mom's lap, I saw her smiling face and felt a new sense of freedom. At that moment in time, I knew I'd never bite anyone ever again.

Letting go of those feelings of mistrust was risky business for me because it necessitated courage. While I've never thought of myself as being brave, I somehow found the nerve on that day to make a change in my life. As a result of my behavior, Kessen forgave me for the Ring Toy Caper,

We were friends again.

and I was ready to begin learning how to be a proper assistance dog with the folks. I won't say that I never did anything wrong ever again because I lapsed a few times into misbehavior, but nothing from that day on was ever done that involved the use of my teeth in an unfriendly manner. Saying goodbye to aggressive behavior was fortunate because my new, big-dog teeth were huge...

Months later, Kessen reminded me of the moment I decided to trust the folks. While I was away in advanced training, he often accompanied them to schools for presentations. During those presentations to the students, our mom and dad always talked about the moment I decided to take a risk and trust them. Not only was it a significant moment for the folks, it changed my life as well. Learning to trust was a risky business, but the rewards were worth the effort.

8

Road Trip

The folks were planning a road trip to Charlotte, North Carolina with Kessen to visit friends, and because I was six months old and fairly obedient, they decided to take me along on the trip. A few years ago, our mom met a woman named Jan through the service organization that gave the pups to puppy raisers across the country. When our mom was raising Kessen, Jan was raising Kessen's sister named Kelyn. While each trained their pups in different parts of the country, Mom and Jan exchanged something called e-mails regarding the pups' similarities, differences, training techniques and anything involved with the growing pups. Jan was a Certified Dog Trainer and knew all about puppy behavior and training. My mom knew a lot as well but wasn't certified as a trainer. She just kept a few paw steps ahead of us, and we never knew what to expect. Therefore, proper behavior was a requirement in our house because no one liked surprises...especially hers!

Kessen and Kelyn were both puppies from the K Litter. The six puppies born into that litter were given names beginning with the letter K and were the result of mixing two great breeds...the Golden Retriever and the Labrador Retriever. Because of this combination, the pups shared characteristics of both breeds. In terms of their similarities, both Kelyn and Kessen were sensitive, willing to learn and loved being in or around water. On the other paw, Kessen had short hair that favored the Labrador Retriever side while Kelyn favored the Golden Retriever side with her long, flowing coat. Kessen was the only pup in his litter with short hair and had a black, nickel-sized spot of fur on his side. Those two characteristics were his and his alone which set him apart from his littermates.

In any event, through months of communications, Mom and Jan became e-mail and phone friends. This trip enabled them to meet each other face to face for the first time and promised to be quite thrilling for both of them.

We were all excited about taking the trip...especially Kessen. He hadn't seen his sister since he was a puppy in California and was extremely anxious to see her again. He wanted to bring his smelly ring toy on the trip to show Kelyn that he had kept it, but the folks wouldn't allow him to have that toy in the car while traveling in very hot weather. The toy had a distinct aroma that permeated an area in lethal ways within seconds. Spending two days traveling in a car with that object would be detrimental to our senses let alone the aromas that would permanently permeate their clothes and our coats. What sort of first impression would we make if we all smelled like the filthy ring toy? Those people wouldn't allow us past their driveway let alone in their house smelling like that toy. Needless to say, the ring toy remained in the toy box at home.

The day came for us to begin our journey to Charlotte, North Carolina, and excitement levels were high. The station wagon, fondly referred to as the Blue Baron due to its dark, blue color and regal appearance, was packed with luggage as well as gifts for Jan and her family. Kessen occupied the back seat while I was in my traveling canvas crate. Mom rode in the passenger seat in front, and Dad was the sole driver due to his enjoyment of driving while behind the

The Blue Baron was ready for the highway!

wheel of the sturdy and reliable Blue Baron.

I was a great car traveler, never got sick in the car and really enjoyed seeing the sights through the intimidating mesh of the canvas crate. Having my teeth caught in that menacing mesh a few months ago was an experience that I will never forget, but my car-riding enthusiasm didn't carry over to Kessen. He, on the other paw, did not enjoy riding in a car at all. Because he was not confined to a crate, he was free to move about in the back seat of the car while wearing a safety harness. He had ample opportunities to view the scenery from all sides of the car. Instead of sitting upright in the middle of the back seat where the view was perfect on all sides, he'd jump into the corner of the back seat while Mom or Dad fastened his safety harness to the seat belt. Then, he assumed a down position on the seat and stared at the car door during the entire trip. The only time he stood up was to change directions and stare at the door on the opposite side. When asked about this odd behavior, he didn't have a reason for what I called his Fear of Car Windows Syndrome, but I promised him that one day, I'd help him move past that fear. His typical response for some of my promises was to roll his eyes and laugh. He did just that when he heard my promise of assistance for the window concerns because I was usually the one needing help.

After two days of driving, we finally pulled into the driveway of Jan's house in North Carolina and saw them waiting for us. We were all very excited as Mom and Jan met and exchanged hugs. Dad and her husband Don shook hands and immediately began talking about sports. As Mom opened the car's back door and unhitched Kessen, he lunged out of the car and happily jumped around everyone. He was either excited to meet everyone or happy to end his staring at the car door. I wasn't sure of his motives and personally didn't care because I was momentarily forgotten in the excitement. Once Mom remembered that I was still in the car, she released me from my crate and allowed me to join the excitement of that first meeting. It was, in my opinion, controlled chaos, but everyone was having fun.

The folks formally introduced us to their new friends, and because they welcomed us with lots of hugs and kisses,

Kessen and I immediately decided to call them Auntie Jan and Uncle Don. Then, we went into the house and were instantly pushed back by a pack of dogs running after each other as if they were on the track of the Indy 500 Race. The barking, howling and screeching reached high pitch levels as these dogs sprinted and turned corners like race cars on rails. All of these dogs running together was what I really considered an authentic pack, and Kessen needed to take note of that fact. His trying to pass the two of us off as a real pack was a bit funny…to say the least.

Anyway, the first time the dogs passed us, they were a complete blur because of their speed. They raced through the music room, made a fast turn into the kitchen, sped through the living room and repeated the cycle at full speed. In the lead and a few paw steps ahead of the pack was a beautiful, honey-colored retriever followed by a regal-looking taller dog. Running in third position was a cream-colored retriever and, in last position but catching up with the pack, was a rather small, spaniel-like mixed breed. The make-up of this pack was quite a unique combination of breeds. While the noise was ear-piercing, their continued race through the house was a sight to behold.

Kessen and I just maintained our positions by the door as the dogs flew by when suddenly, the Golden Retriever, who led the pack, snapped up a fly right out of the air while running at full speed. According to Kessen, Kelyn was the only dog he had ever known who could do that. As he witnessed that fly catching triumph, Kessen wondered if that gorgeous dog might be his sister Kelyn. He whispered her name softly in hopes that he might actually be seeing her for the first time in years. Because a dog's hearing is so much better than their human counterparts, the lead dog immediately stopped in her tracks when she heard her name. That stopping action on her part caused all of the dogs following her to crash into each other. Not even caring about the commotion she caused, the Golden Retriever came

We were together again!

over to take a look at Kessen. Checking him out from every angle, she stopped as she saw the black, nickel-shaped patch of fur on his side. When they were puppies in California, she called that spot his doorbell. Looking into his eyes, she knew that she was looking into the eyes of her dear brother

Kessen. After many years of being apart, they were together again.

After a lot of sniffing and snuggling, Kelyn introduced Kessen to the members of her pack and then invited me to join in the fun. The race through the house was on again at full speed. As usual, I was last in the pack. The larger dogs were fast runners, but I could have beaten that little mixed breed. His tiny little legs were moving as if battery powered, but I knew I could easily pass him. However, being newly invited into to the pack, racing past him wasn't at all appropriate. Linus would have been proud of my decision to adhere to proper pack etiquette. After all, we were guests in this house and had to put our best paws forward so as not to embarrass our folks.

Although we were exhausted after all of that racing around, something happened that was most unusual. Without any warning, Auntie Jan stepped right in front of the speeding pack, extended her arms and in a most self-assured voice told us to stop running. Since I was having so much fun running around the rooms of the house, the thought of ending the race never crossed my mind. However, the other dogs abruptly stopped in their tracks which caused them to crash into each other in front of Auntie Jan. I only slowed down to avoid the massive canine collision.

Seeing these dogs respond in that manner made me momentarily rethink this leader of the pack system. Based upon what just happened, Kelyn apparently wasn't the real leader of the pack at all...Auntie Jan was! The pile-up of dogs in front of her was proof that while Kelyn held a prominent position, she was actually second in command.

All eyes were on Auntie Jan.

Even though I was thoroughly confused by what just happened, time stood still for all of us as Auntie Jan stood silently in the middle of the room with all eyes focused on her. I had never seen anything like it. All of these dogs, sitting upright with their eyes glued on this formidable figure, actually formed an organized pack with a real leader. What was surprising was that the pack leader wasn't a dog at all! Auntie Jan was in charge and not one dog, sitting silently in that room, was going to challenge her position. Believe me, I sat down very quickly after witnessing that strange turn of events.

I was fascinated by this woman's complete control over all of the canines in the room, and she never once raised her voice. She introduced us to the members of her pack, and now we had names to match the pack members. Kelyn, the honey-colored Golden Retriever, was her second in command and Kessens's sister. The regal, black and tan Gordon Setter was Sidney, and the glamorous, light-colored English Cream Golden Retriever was named Carly. I definitely had to talk to her about her grooming regimen since I thoroughly envied the condition of her shiny coat and impeccably trimmed nails. Beppe, a color combination of browns and blacks, was the Cavalier King Charles Spaniel-Dachshund mix and was asleep with his eyes open while

This was a real pack!

sitting upright. I had never seen that before either. This trip was turning into a treat bowl full of new experiences.

Something in Auntie Jan's demeanor connected with all of us on a canine level, and she had complete control of

93

the pack. At that moment, I wanted to be just like her and briefly imagined myself being the leader of my very own pack. All my canine members would bow down before me and answer to my every bark and howl. I was completely lost in a glorious stretch of my imagination and would have continued if Kessen hadn't noticed my being engaged in a fantasy. He discreetly nudged me out of my daydream, and I quickly rejoined the group's attentive stance. Knowing that I'd never be in a leadership position such as in my day dream, I would remember this moment for the rest of my life.

Auntie Jan released us to play a bit more with each other. Soon, it was time to leave and check into the hotel for the night. Because everyone was exhausted from the excitement of the day, we were all eager to get some sleep. Tomorrow held the promise of new adventures since we were all going to a barbecue in another state...South Carolina. Kessen and I didn't really know what a barbecue was, but it didn't matter since it meant that we would see our new canine friends once again. Tomorrow couldn't come soon enough.

We got up very early in anticipation of this next trip and were surprised that we were all going in one vehicle. Uncle Don was driving, and Dad was riding in the passenger seat. Mom and Auntie Jan were in the back seat while I sat on Auntie Jan's lap. Personally, I thought my position was the best seat in the car. Kessen and Kelyn, sharing stories of their lives, were behind us in the cargo area. Because they were exhausted from yesterday's excitement, Carly, Sidney and Beppe remained at their home.

The drive to the barbecue in South Carolina didn't take very long at all. When we reached our destination, Uncle Don drove the car into a long driveway leading to a beautiful house. Auntie Jan took Kelyn and Kessen from the cargo area while Mom had me leashed closely by her side as we walked to the backyard of the house. When we got to the gate, we saw people relaxing in lawn chairs as well as a large group of dogs of all colors, ages and sizes racing around the yard. As soon as the gate opened, Auntie Jan and Uncle Don introduced our folks to their friends and let us loose to join the other dogs.

At first, we weren't sure which way to run because the dogs weren't running in any sort of pattern. So, we just joined in when we saw a vacant space in the group. The dogs were mostly older or near Kessen's age. As I looked around the yard, I spotted a pup sitting by the flowers and knew I found my playmate for the day. This pup was about my age, a bit darker in color but, once she saw me, ran to greet me in a most spirited way. Her name

She was the perfect playmate!

was Milani, and after appropriate sniffing, we ran off together to explore the huge yard.

While Kessen and Kelyn were running all over the place with the older dogs, Milani and I raced circles around the yard in search of mischief. It didn't take long before we found the perfect opportunity for potential mischief. Day lilies of all colors and sizes lined the white fence that enclosed the yard. Milani and I looked at each other and immediately knew those flowers needed a haircut. With the precision of a buzz saw, we trimmed the blossoms of those day lilies before anyone noticed our actions. Leaving only the stems intact, we regrettably never felt any remorse over what we had just done. Fortunately for us, no one seemed to observe those mischievous acts. While it certainly wasn't the best way for visitors to behave, sometimes puppies just can't help being puppies. While that reasoning might not hold up in a canine court, it was the best Milani and I had to offer at the time. We did, however, pay the price for our mischievous behavior later in the day when our digestive systems rebelled against the onslaught of day lilies in our stomachs. Everything came with a price which proved there was no such thing as a free lunch!

We were pups gone wild!

Because of our chaotic running around, we had to relax for quite a while before eating our dinners. Each of the dogs found a comfortable place in the cool grass and either slept or just watched the people fully enjoying each other's company. The folks sat around a huge table that offered hotdogs, hamburgers, chicken, a variety of salads, breads and sweet-smelling desserts. The delightful aromas that filled the air were mouthwatering and bordered on cruelty since all we had to look forward to was a bowl of dry dog food.

On the plus side, I finally learned that a barbecue was a social event where people sat in comfortable lawn chairs, talked to each other and enjoyed delicious meals from a decorated buffet table. The canine guests, on the other paw, ran enthusiastically around an enormous yard, had the opportunity to see and smell delicious food and ate dry dog food from a bowl. Dogs were unquestionably at a distinct disadvantage in this type of social event.

I had the best seat in the house.

As the sun set, all of the guests relaxed and chatted with each other in the comfort of the colorful lawn chairs. Kessen and Kelyn sat off to the side exchanging funny experiences, and I decided to spend some time with Dad. As he sat talking with a woman from Auntie Jan's group, he welcomed my approach with open arms and gently positioned me on his lap. I had a great view of all of the people as well as the dogs resting contentedly in the grass after eating. As I looked around, the woman sitting next to us called out to her dog. The dog was a stunning Golden Retriever who was relaxing with a few of the other dogs at the far end of the yard. As the dog approached us, I couldn't help but stare at her because she looked so familiar. The woman called her Lulu, and she looked remarkably like Linus…only his coat was golden in color while hers was quite blonde.

Unlike Linus, she seemed a bit shy, but the resemblance to him was uncanny. Dad even noticed the likeness and mentioned that a dog named Linus had stayed at our house to teach puppy etiquette and looked amazingly like Lulu. After Dad and Lulu's mom exchanged additional information about the two dogs, they concluded that Linus and Lulu were actually brother and sister. The odds of meeting her, let alone at a barbecue in South Carolina, were

What a coincidence!

astronomical, yet here she was. As it turned out, Lulu and Linus were both puppies from the L Litter, born in California a few years ago and sent to various parts of the country for their training as potential assistance dogs. When the pups were eight weeks old, Linus was sent to a woman in the state of Illinois for training, and Lulu went to the family in South Carolina.

Dad put me down on the grass so I might spend some time with Lulu. She was just as surprised as I was about the coincidence and wanted to know everything about her brother. I was proud to tell her that he specialized in teaching puppy etiquette to unruly pups and was known as The Big Gun because of his unique teaching techniques. I never mentioned that he was called to our house because of my behavior but was sure to mention that he had visited the house for Kessen when he was young. There was no need to let her know that I was a ruffian as a pup needing outside counsel from her brother.

As Lulu and I shared experiences about Linus, Dad and Lulu's owner continued their conversations about the two dogs. It was just such an uncanny coincidence, and Dad promised to tell Linus' owner all about meeting Lulu. Dad wanted to take a picture of Lulu to share with Linus' owner when we got home. As he focused the camera on her beautiful face, Lulu turned her face to the side just as Linus always did when someone attempted to take his picture. Wasn't it interesting that both

Lulu looked away.

dogs shared that same mannerism when having pictures taken? This day was just filled with surprises!

Kessen and Kelyn wandered over to us, and both dogs were excited to meet Lulu. Kessen told her what a wonderful brother she had and how much he learned from him. Fortunately for me, Kessen didn't go into specifics about Linus' reasons for being at our house. Breathing a sigh of relief, I was happy that my reputation was safe for the moment.

As we were getting ready to leave, I said goodbye to Lulu and told her how happy I was to have met her. She, in turn, was just as happy to have met me and learn all about her dear brother Linus. Milani awakened from her nap and rushed across the yard to say goodbye to me. While we knew we'd probably never meet again, we enjoyed sharing

the day together...except for the day lily escapade that continued to wreak havoc with our digestive systems. But, coming to this barbecue was great fun for all.

Milani came to say goodbye.

We piled into the car and assumed somewhat similar positions for the journey back to Auntie Jan's and Uncle Don's house. Kessen and Kelyn immediately fell fast asleep in the cargo area. Due to exhaustion from the day's events, I changed sitting positions from the earlier car ride and was draped over my mom's lap like a rag doll. Tomorrow we would begin our journey home, but all was not lost because each of us had such a good time on this trip.

The folks finally met and shared quality time with their new friends...not just in North Carolina but in South Carolina as well. Mom and Auntie Jan were so happy to finally see each other and would continue to send those things called e-mails in the days and years to come. Kessen and I had the uncanny experience of connecting and spending time with Lulu. Kessen thoroughly enjoyed his reunion with Kelyn, and I had a fantastic time with Milani. In addition to those awesome experiences, I encountered an authentic leader of a canine pack. Auntie Jan rocked! This was the best road trip ever taken...

When I saw how Auntie Jan maintained control of her canine pack, I lapsed into the fantasy of one day being a pack leader. At the time, I knew it was just a silly, puppy's daydream. Little did I know that years later, Kessen would give that leadership position to me when he retired. While I wanted to be like Auntie Jan and joked about it with Kessen, I realized as I got older what a great leader Kessen was and what a difficult job he had with me in his pack. My hope was to live up to his expectations while remaining totally glamorous!

9

The Glamour Gal

Even as a very young puppy, my appearance was really important to me. I'd see my reflection in a puddle and imagine how I'd look when I got older. My brother Bart always told me that I was the cutest puppy of the litter, but he was biased because he was my favorite brother and always talked about my petite size, almond-shaped dark brown eyes and extremely curly eyelashes. My having a fluffy, blonde coat was an advantage in the likeability department because everyone knew that blondes have more fun!

Looking good was important.

While puppies weren't typically preoccupied with their looks, my attention to my appearance totally governed my actions during the day and made me different from my other siblings. They didn't care a bit about how dirty their bodies got while rolling in the dirt or how their muddy paws left paw prints on the floor when they ran into the house at mealtime. They just ate when food was available, played when it was convenient and had fun whenever the opportunity arose.

I, on the other paw, thought it was very important to

always present a clean appearance...especially at meal time. Let's be serious...we weren't raised by savages. We had a wonderful mother who tried to teach us rules of puppy etiquette, and those rules included puppy hygiene. I wasn't a bit interested in running around in the rain, sliding through mud holes or showing up for meals with dirt, sticks and grass hanging out of my ears. As far as I was concerned, that lack of cleanliness just wasn't an acceptable appearance at the food bowl. In addition to their messy appearances, those puppies attacked that food bowl with a vengeance. Who wanted to eat while surrounded by a bunch of dirty puppies who foraged around the food bowl like feral beasts? In my opinion, mealtimes were supposed to be treated with respect and politeness. Instead, mealtimes turned into Come As You Are and Feed Your Face As Fast As You Can events that occurred three times a day.

My siblings felt differently about my views on mealtime decorum and often made fun of my attention to any form of etiquette. I never joined them when they danced around in puddles following a rain storm or chased frogs that hopped in and out of the water around the pond behind the house. Those activities offered the most opportunities for getting dirty, and thoughts of behaving in such a manner made me cringe. If I had my way, the pads of my paws would never touch anything wet or dirty.

Some of my littermates thought my attitude toward cleanliness and appearances made me snobbish, but I didn't mind their criticisms. They were mean to me anyway due to my birth order, so their taunts about my puppy hygiene had no effect on me. Being clean and well-groomed was just evidence of being true to myself, and I handled anything and everything they dished out.

When I came to the new house, complete with a new family, I figured they'd appreciate my quest for maintaining good grooming standards. Seeing me avoid puddles after a rainfall, not rolling around in dirt or eating delicately from the food bowl amazed them. Please don't misunderstand… I loved to eat, but eating slowly was a sign of good breeding as well as great for the digestive system. Apparently, no other puppy, who came to their house, maintained such high standards of restraint at the food bowl as well as the attention to cleanliness. I was, in a sense, an oddity to them in many ways.

Even though I sensed that Kessen was already caring for me because he liked me and not just because I was forced upon him as his little sister, he often thought my quest for perfection and femininity was a bit superficial. We just had

He loved his baby pool.

opposite opinions about things...such as water. I, personally, loved a nice cool drink of water on a warm day but had no interest at all in being given a bath. Kessen, on the other paw, would hang around the bath tub staring at it as if by focusing his eyes on the tub, the folks would give him a bath. He was always the first one to jump into the baby pool our dad put in the yard for us during the summer. Kessen would jump in and out of the pool and attempt to empty it by kicking up his hind legs. Seeing Dad unwind the hose from the hose reel sent Kessen into a frenzy. He'd frantically run around the yard while waiting for our dad to water the flowers so he could jump through the water streaming from the hose or grab a gulp of water while flying through the air. Kessen's fascination with water was extremely peculiar.

When our folks took him for a Fun Swim at a nearby hydrotherapy center before he went off to advanced training, Kessen swam so hard that he caused a problem with his tail. The next day, the folks had to take him to the veterinarian because his tail was limp, and he was whimpering in pain. The

Kessen could swim all day.

veterinarian diagnosed Kessen as having Limber Tail Syndrome and put him on antibiotics for a few days. Eventually, his tail went back to its normal wagging, but he wasn't a happy dog for a while.

Now, one would think that an experience like that would deter him from future, similar endeavors. Not so with our esteemed pack leader. A few years later, Kessen repeated the swimming frenzy in a different location, but Mom, knowing her dog's love for the world of water, came prepared for his foolishness by bringing his medication.

His escapades with water were in direct opposition to mine. If I saw any indication of a bath in my future, I made myself scarce somewhere in the house. I deliberately kept clean to avoid such activities, but eventually I'd end up in the tub. At least, I'd have the scent of light lavender on my body when the bath was over, but I refused to enjoy the bath itself. When it was my turn for the Fun Swim, I never even got down the ramp into the water. I planted my paws on the

tiled walkway next to the pool and refused to enter. The assistants tried tossing various toys into the water to get me to move down the ramp, but I wouldn't budge. Even the scent of dried liver treats wouldn't get me into that pool. Recognizing that the Fun Swim was both unwanted and stressful for me, the folks just took me home...dry as a

My worst nightmare...

bone left out in the summer sunshine!

The first sight of moisture on the deck leading to the dog run deterred me from going outside. The slightest bit of rainfall kept me in the house until it stopped, and the deck dried. I was extremely fortunate that the size of my bladder accommodated my eccentricity. In my mind, there was just something unnatural about getting the pads of my paws wet. I don't know when that particular quirk began, but I have never been able to overcome it. Truth be told, I never tried either. Perhaps that peculiarity was just part of my relentless quest for cleanliness. Every time it rained or a bit of moisture appeared on the deck, Kessen knew I wasn't about to go outside. He just looked at me, rolled his eyes and laughed.

After my adventure in advanced training, the family planned a well-earned vacation. Our mom's dream was to rent a house right on the beach off the coast of North Carolina, and that's exactly what she and my dad did. Kessen was really excited because of the beach aspect. I, on the other paw, was not as enthusiastic.

North Carolina, here we come!

In preparation for the experience, Mom bought very expensive life vests for us since safety is an important factor when swimming in the ocean. First of all, the vests were a hideous shade of orange that I'm sure glowed in the dark. Secondly, the dull, brown trim added insult to injury with its lack of fashion sense. I believed the combination of colors made me look quite pale and did nothing to bring out the highlights in my eyes.

As a side note, there is a common misconception among humans that dogs aren't able to see and distinguish colors. While we may not see colors as definitively as they do, we can and do, however, have our very own way of recognizing shades of colors. Why do you think we balk at the strange way people dress us on holidays?

Anyway, I had no intention of wearing the vest in public unless forced to do so. The color palette was totally wrong for me, and I had no intention of going anywhere near the water. What was Mom thinking when she bought those vests? Kessen loved his vest and couldn't wait to wear it when we reached our vacation destination. I blame some of his lack of fashion sense on being comfortable with having that pink nose.

Off we went on that special vacation and drove for days in really hot weather. Even with the air conditioning blasting in the car, everyone was sweating. We made numerous stops at fast food restaurants along the way so the folks could get some wet paper towels for cooling our heads. Both in and out of the car was like traveling in a blast furnace! The heat in that part of the country was extreme, and none of us had ever experienced temperatures as severe before this trip. Anyway, we finally got to the beach house, and it was more beautiful than anyone imagined. The house was huge, had fenced upper and lower decks, a barbecue grill, lounge chairs and was located right on the beach. Mom's dream came true, and my nightmare began.

Our Aunties, also good friends as well as our puppy sitters, came along with us to enjoy the great, sunny beach experience. After everyone settled in, Mom put Kessen's vest on him, fastened his lengthy tether complete with identification tags and declared his readiness for some beach fun. Kessen, attached to our dad by a tether for safety in the ocean, bolted out of the door, ran down the boardwalk, jumped onto the hot sand and almost dragged Dad into the water. The ocean's waves were calling to Kessen, and all he could do was answer the invitation as quickly as possible.

Our Aunties were special.

My experience, on the other paw, was quite different. I stood patiently while our mom put that hideous vest on me, waited while my tether was attached, began the trek out the door and walked down the boardwalk to the end of my journey. That's right...the end of my journey. Reaching the step leading down onto the sand was as far as I was going to go. I assumed a sitting position at the edge of the step knowing that these paws of mine were never going to feel the sand between the pads of my paws much less venture into the ocean. Mom tried every technique for luring me onto the sand and near the water, but her efforts were in vain since I wasn't going anywhere. Aside from the fact that the ocean was such an immense and intimidating expanse of water, I just didn't like getting wet.

Mom wasn't going to force me to do something that might prove stressful for me, so she just sat down next to me on the stair and watched Kessen make a fool of himself in the water. Since Mom knew I wasn't fond of water, she left the store's purchase tag on my vest so she would be able to return it when we got home. She also knew that Kessen would eventually over work his tail in the water, so she brought his medication. Those meds sure came in handy that evening. Although Kessen was in a bit of pain, he'd find his way to the ocean again in the morning.

The week at the beach proved to be quite relaxing for

Kessen's idea of a good time…

all involved. The folks, the Aunties and Kessen swam in the ocean during the day, and I watched their antics while sunning myself on the upper deck of the beach house. In the

evening, we would all meet on the upper deck for dinner. The folks and the Aunties would relax in comfortable chairs while Kessen and I enjoyed watching the area residents walking their dogs along the beach. Some lucky dogs were even allowed to splash around in the water. Kessen reminded me of

My idea of a good time…   the fun I was missing by not going

for a *splash and dive* as he called it. He wanted me to join in the fun on the beach so he could call me his Beach Blanket Blondie. Like that was ever going to happen! I just allowed him to babble on as I sat with the others and watched the sun go down. Seeing that vibrant sun descending and disappearing beyond the horizon every evening was a spectacular sight worth remembering. While I managed never to get my paws wet, the beach house escapade was a wonderful way to spend the week and became one of the best vacations I ever had.

Because of Kessen's frequent escapades in the ocean, he desperately needed a bath...a very long bath. Even though he was hosed down after each jaunt in the ocean, it wasn't the same as having a bath. Since I was riding in the back seat next to him on the way home, having the windows open a bit was a blessing. There is nothing worse than a smelly dog who loves to cuddle, and the folks would be in for a real treat if they didn't bathe Kessen as soon as we got home. That being said, giving Kessen a bath was the top priority once we entered the house...even before bringing in the luggage from the car. Since I didn't go on the sand and never ventured near the ocean, I was just as clean as when we started the trip.

Once we got home, I was able to resume attention to my appearance. The glass doors leading to the decks at the beach house never gave me a clear view of my facial tones. However, the patio doors here at home were crystal clear and gave me that fresh, daylight view of myself that I checked every once in a while. My evening facial check was reserved for looking at my reflection in the oven door since it gave my face a bit of a candlelight glow. Was I much too preoccupied with my personal appearance as Kessen often mentioned? If that were true, why would he now call me his

Glamour Gal? As far as I was concerned, Kessen's nickname for me was both accurate and appropriate.

Following Kessen's bathing ritual, the family resumed the casual routine of the household. Kessen, once again, assumed his duties as pack leader in a most stately manner, and I found great enjoyment in the memories of the beach house escapade as well as great consolation in knowing that I was never a Beach Blanket Blondie. That nickname might have given Kessen fodder for teasing me for a long, long time. Personally, being his Glamour Gal was the most appropriate nickname and not only described me perfectly but suited me just fine...

In Kessen's version of the beach house escapade, he didn't spend too much time on my refusal to accept the beach environment as a wild and wonderful experience. Sitting on the last step on the boardwalk while watching Kessen dive into the water, I saw a very different dog. He wasn't the strict pack leader who lived by rules and regulations while at home. Here, on the coast of North Carolina, he was a dog who threw caution to the wind and enjoyed life to the fullest...risking Limber Tail Syndrome once again just to enjoy splashing in the ocean's waves. Gotta give him a lot of credit for that!

10

College Prep

When I first came to live with my new family, Kessen set a few minutes aside each day for my participation in his Puppy Training Seminars. During those sessions, he shared

This sounded like important stuff.

words of wisdom regarding all aspects of my training as a future assistance dog. Stressing the importance of both emotional and physical preparation, Kessen reminded me of my responsibilities regarding learning new commands, walking appropriately on a leash and acquiring various techniques for greetings in public. All elements of the assistance training program would take me on an amazing journey filled with new experiences, provide a treat bag full of excitement as well as lend insights into the future goal of helping others. According to Kessen, everything I learned and accomplished during the next twelve months would prepare me for entrance to Puppy College. I wasn't sure what he was talking about in terms of going to some type of college for puppies, but the thought of having new and exciting adventures was just what this puppy fancied. However, the part about helping others was a total surprise for me and completely foreign to my nature.

From a very early age, I had a tendency to put my needs first. As superficial as it sounded, I was only being true to myself. Perhaps my being pint-sized, having almond-shaped eyes as dark as chocolate with exceptionally long and curly eyelashes gave me a bit of a vulnerable appearance and might have led other dogs to believe that I needed rescuing. For whatever reasons, dogs just took care of me, and I welcomed their assistance as well as the attention.

When I was living in California for the first eight weeks of my life, my brother Bart defended me on a daily basis and insured my safety when bothered by my siblings. After traveling to my new home in the Midwest, Kessen, learning of his big brother status, immediately assumed a protective role in my life.

Big brother responsibilities also involved helping me overcome fears encountered in day to day experiences. When I was fearful of going down the basement stairs for the first time, Kessen came to my rescue and demonstrated how to successfully complete that task by going up and down the stairs while I watched. However, his repeatedly doing that demo didn't make those stairs look any less

Not going to do it!

threatening. While he was on the way down for the third time, in what I considered a dangerous descent, I quickly disappeared into another room. Was I being ungrateful by totally ignoring his efforts to help me? Probably so, but in my defense, his going up and down so easily didn't make those stairs any less threatening to me. A few days later when I felt a bit more courageous, I remembered his techniques for descending the stairs and successfully completed the

exercise. Although applied at a later date, his efforts to help me were not in vain. My risking the staircase exercise based upon Kessen's demonstrations proved, beyond a doubt, that I valued his assistance.

Rufus was my first love.

I willingly admit that having Kessen's readiness to protect me, in effect, isolated me from solving everyday situations. My very first encounter with puppy love made Kessen very uneasy because he wanted to guard me from possible heartache. Rufus, a Jack Russell Terrier having the reputation of being a real dog's dog, was the first object of my affection as well as the reason for my future heartache in the realm of puppy love.

Sad to say, Rufus and I shared a rather brief romance. While volunteering in the Reading with Rover program at the library, Rufus and I stared at each other from opposite

His look was intoxicating.

corners of the room while children read to us. It was a bit of a disservice to the children, but they weren't aware of our romantic aspirations and continued to read on as we stared like star-crossed lovers into each other's eyes. Rufus and I also attended a few gift-wrapping gigs at a

We worked well together.

neighboring book store and shared love-sick looks at each other amidst the paper, ribbons and tape. We were both on the roller coaster of love. However, anyone who has ever ridden on a roller coaster knows that the ride eventually comes to an end.

Our roller coaster ride of love ended at one of our assisted therapy group's fund-raising events in the park. I was unexpectedly dumped by Rufus for a chestnut-colored Cavalier King Charles Spaniel named Daisy. Even though she and I were both exceptional representatives of our individual breeds, my long, curly eyelashes and almond-shaped eyes were no competition for this dainty canine with her exquisite, plume-like tail. Watching Rufus' head swing back and forth as he followed the movement of Daisy's tail made me question the authenticity of that amazing tail. How could a dog that small have such an enormous, beautifully-shaped tail? Deciding that she must use tail extensions to make her tail look fuller and more attractive lessened the heartache from being dumped by Rufus. At least with me, what you see is what you get!

Kessen was livid when he heard that I was dumped by Rufus and threatened to take him behind the fund-raising booth and give him a piece of his mind. However, I insisted that Kessen not get involved because his losing even a few brain cells was a risky move on a number of levels. Kessen needed every bit of the brain

Kessen wanted to protect me again.

matter crammed into that cranial container called his brain, and someone had to protect that remarkable brain of his. Now, it was my turn to protect him.

Besides, Rufus was just being true to himself. Since he was handsome, a player and real dog's dog, the canines of the female persuasion fell for him every time. Let's face it...Rufus was a Babe Magnet who radiated an element of danger, and that possibility made him totally irresistible. Based upon my request, Kessen just let the situation play out as it was destined to happen.

Rufus and I parted ways in a somewhat friendly manner...agreeing to no hard feelings on either side. I was definitely hurt by the experience but wouldn't dare let Rufus know how I felt. Weeks later, I heard that Daisy dumped Rufus for a German Shepherd working with the Bomb and Arson Squad. I secretly experienced a tinge of satisfaction

Kessen always helped me.

with that bit of information. In moving from a dog who radiated danger to one who faced danger on a daily basis, Daisy proved herself to be a true player and most impressive adversary in my eyes. Under very different circumstances, we might even have been friends.

Having canines always taking care of me was a great source of enjoyment as well as a possible motive for not being open to helping others as a career. Kessen, assuming his big brother position on a higher level, just did things for me without my even asking for help. For example, our folks insisted that we pick up our toys at the end of the day. Kessen would meander around the house, grab his toys from the floor and drop them into the toy box. If I mentioned having an exhausting day in public, Kessen would immediately run around the house, gather my toys and complete the toy clean-up requirement for me. Now, did I flutter my long, curly eyelashes, slowly blink my eyes and yawn politely when mentioning my tiring day? Perhaps I did, but once again, I was just acting in accordance with the nurturing done by others. In a vague sense, I was a victim of over protection.

There were times, however, when curly eyelashes and enticing glances didn't get the job done in terms of doing my bidding. Sometimes, I actually had to commit blatant acts just to get my way. A perfect example of that was my ability to have a credible temper tantrum at the drop of a treat. It worked more on dogs than on the folks, but that fact didn't stop me from the challenge. Both Kessen, as well as the folks, fell prey to that scheme of mine more than once.

I had a secret weapon.

On one occasion, I performed my most flamboyant temper tantrum while my mom and I were in line waiting to purchase some books at a book store. I was bored and missing my meal time, so I just assumed a down position, turned over on my back, kicked my legs up and screeched at the top of my lungs. What I considered my finest moment in Tantrum Land went unnoticed by my mom. She just continued to look at a display of cards and completely ignored my shrieking and howling. The store's customers watched and thought my tantrum was a bit funny. To add insult to injury, when all was said and done, I was still in that silly line with my mom waiting for her purchases. My tantrums didn't work as well with humans…especially with our mom and dad.

Kessen, on the other paw, fell for it almost every time. The folks periodically provided a variety of suitable toys for us. We usually had the choice of either a squeaky toy, a scented rope toy that guaranteed teeth cleaning or a rubber bone that contained a treat. Since most of the squeaky toys

Kessen always got first choice.

seemed suitable for a younger puppy and my teeth were already brilliantly white, I preferred the toys with the treats...as did Kessen. Now, the folks, observing the pack order, always gave Kessen the first choice of toys, and that's when the problem occurred. He would always grab the toy containing the treat leaving me with the choice of either the soft, squeaky toy meant for a puppy or the canine version of dental floss in the rope toy.

Losing the opportunity for the rubber bone with the treat sent me into my tantrum mode. I'd position myself next to Kessen as he chewed on that bone, turn over on my back, kick up my legs and start screeching. Kessen, having

a sensitive nature, would either tolerate my screeching or drop the bone and leave the room. Each time I played the tantrum card, I had a fifty-fifty chance of getting that rubber bone from Kessen. Because I liked those odds, it was worth the challenge. Of course, there were also times when, in the midst of my screeching, Kessen would drop

The Get-Me Gimme-Girl

the bone after he had eaten the treat and leave the room. Somehow in my twisted notion of fair play, I thought his dropping that toy after eating the treat was cheating.

When I used my feminine wiles to get my way or have things done for me, Kessen often called me his Get-Me Gimme-Girl. Since he took his role as big brother quite seriously, he was quite the pushover for my lady-like biddings. However, he just didn't understand that dogs, who didn't even know me, seemed to want to help. Let's face it...I somehow had this aura that drew dogs to me much like a magnet. They couldn't help themselves in terms of wanting to help me, and I got used to that sort of treatment on a daily basis.

Telling me about my future journey having new experiences and excitement was encouraging, but how was

I ever going to be successful in a career as an assistance dog? I had no basis for that type of endeavor and, to be honest, didn't think it was in my best interest to pursue it. However, I really didn't have much choice...or did I?

The folks, fulfilling their roles as puppy raisers by preparing me for this Puppy College gig, filled my days with fun, training and surprises around every corner. As the weeks turned into months, the simple walks in the neighborhood and visits to nearby parks progressed to trips to restaurants, schools, shopping malls, hospitals, concerts and church services. At times, the routine was quite rigorous, but those public outings led to people commenting on how well-trained I was or more importantly, how pretty I was. The career goal of helping others was overshadowed by the fun and attention received from my admiring public.

When on outings, I always wore my cape that had a patch identifying the canine assistance organization and my potential as a future assistance dog. While a young puppy in training, Kessen thought his cape was magical. Since he believed in this extraordinary power of his cape, he never cared too much about his appearance. I, on the other paw, regarded appearance as being first and foremost of importance while in the

I was dressed for success!

public eye. Wearing my cape and seeing my reflection in the glass door of a restaurant upon entering or in the side view of a glass elevator at a mall gave me a distinct sense of self-confidence in my appearance. While the color of my cape did nothing to offset the softness of my blonde coat, the over-sized fit of the cape actually made my slender body appear fashionably attired. Appearance meant everything to me, and I was hitting all of the marks in the treat bowl of glamour and fashion...gorgeous, slender, well-dressed and runway ready!

Much to the dismay of the folks, there were times when walking properly on a leash just didn't suit me. I had a rebellious streak that surfaced once in a while, and this particular occasion happened to be one of them. While going for a walk in the park, I decided that walking at my mom's side just wasn't working for me. I wasn't enjoying

I didn't see this coming.

that confined experience. So, I took the opportunity to lunge into the grass, zig-zag as far as the leash would allow and then settle down in the weeds. Upon seeing my mom's expression, I immediately realized that my decision to take leash-behavior to a new level wasn't in my best interest.

This was definitely not my mom's first rodeo in terms of puppy training. Faster than a fly caught in mid-air, she pulled a blue, ribbon-like contraption from her pocket. It closely resembled a type of collar, but had more parts to it. Within seconds, I had a fabric strap loosely fastened around my mouth and another clipped around the back of my head. Kessen warned me about this contraption in one of his Puppy Training Seminars, but as usual, I paid little attention to his information.

I was now under the control of the dreaded head collar! According to what

Kessen heard from our mom's presentations, this type of collar dated all the way back to wolf pack behavior. The leader of the wolf pack, referred to as the Alpha, would correct the outranked members of the pack by grabbing their mouths called muzzles and re-directing the members to the desired behavior. This

Kessen's seminars were important.

contraption worked in the same way and reminded the dog that whoever was at the other end of the leash was in total control.

Once again, Kessen was right on track with his information. If I had only listened to his info, my appearance would not be flawed by this contraption of canine conformity. My only hope was that I wouldn't run into any other dogs while wearing this type of collar. My reputation as a well-trained canine in the community would be tarnished. On the plus side, my gear was well coordinated since the head collar matched the trim on my cape. This day's entire leash-walking experience, while embarrassing, reminded me that I had a lot to learn if I wanted to maintain my impeccable appearance in public, and paying attention during Kessen's seminars was of the utmost importance.

Kessen often reminded me of the frivolity of my persistent pursuit of up-to-the minute style, but, as I said many times, I was just being true to myself. As superficial as my commitment to glamour seemed to others, pretending to be serious about a career in assistance just seemed wrong, and I, with some occasional regret, frequently traveled a very thin line between right and wrong. There had to be other ways to help people and not give up my daily pursuit of trendy appearances.

I was sure Kessen would help me find ways to do just that. After all, he was a therapy dog who worked in a library program, played games with autistic children as well as

I was ready to rock the kennels with my flair for beauty.

entertained children in wheel chairs. I could certainly offer help in those settings as a hobby while maintaining my stylish appearance on the home front.

Although I thought about possible alternatives to a total commitment to assistance, the folks were focused on my training and preparation for entering Puppy College. I followed their specialized program as much as possible but just didn't connect with that notion of assistance. Giving service to others was, indeed, a special calling, but as I mentioned before, my personal idea of service was room service…preferably in a five-star doggie-motel! I just had to figure out a way to get my ideas across to the folks.

As the time approached for my leaving for Puppy College, Kessen offered all sorts of advice as preparation for the experience. To be honest, I was excited about going as well as a bit sad to be leaving the house that became my home. I would definitely miss the folks as well as Kessen so much. For the first time in my life, I was going to have to take care of myself, and that fact alone was really a bit daunting. However, I felt totally prepared for this new Puppy College experience because both the folks and Kessen devoted the last twelve months to my college prep training. I was proficient in my

I was totally prepared.

commands, walked nicely on a leash in public without the dreaded head collar and represented the assistance organization in a most favorable way. In addition to those significant accomplishments, I truthfully looked absolutely marvelous! Look out Puppy College, here I come...

Kessen's versions of my early puppy behaviors were extremely kind. He valued his role as big brother and protector so much so that he left out numerous details regarding my quest for glamour and use of manipulation for getting my way. While some might refer to me as the Mistress of Manipulation, which was a most entertaining title, it only described a small part of my personality. Sure, I was obsessed with glamour and, at times, used my chic appearance to get my way, but I wasn't afraid to admit to having those distinctive sides to my character. I was being honest and just being me. Underneath the attention to appearance and flair for fashion sense was a kind, gentle and caring dog...who, as an adult dog, never intentionally hurt anyone and worked at helping others in my own special way. The future events in my life were proof of those qualities and, at the same time, became my legacy. Will I be remembered as a fashionista Labrador Retriever who valued glamour, chic attire and wore an assistance cape well? I certainly hope so!

11

Campus Caper

Kessen's Puppy Training Seminars, dating back to the first day I arrived at the house, were usually pretty dull. However, I'd listen attentively until my eyes glazed over from boredom but was still able to make my body look like I was paying attention to his words of wisdom. The day before I was to enter the advanced training program, Kessen invited me to the final session that dealt with his experiences while at the training facility.

According to Kessen, the advanced training program for potential assistance dogs, lovingly referred to as Puppy College by the canines, was the most rigorous chapter in a future assistance dog's life. The program was designed as a true *make or break* time for the dogs because assistance dogs had to be perfect in terms of temperament, training

Kessen shared his experiences.

and desire. He was extremely clear about the program's expectations, but why in the world did Kessen think this particular program was right for me?

Having lived with me for the past twelve months, did I ever demonstrate any of those characteristics with him? Apparently, Kessen and the folks believed I had undiscovered talents and would benefit from the training program. Perhaps they knew more about me than I knew about myself. What are the odds of that happening?

In preparation for my going, Kessen wanted me to know what he experienced when in the program. He sincerely wanted to be an assistance dog, and while in his college prep program with the folks, he worked tirelessly at perfecting his skills. He was totally prepared, proficient in his commands and had the intense desire to be successful. Even if a dog truly wanted a career in assistance, not all dogs would qualify, and Kessen was one of those dogs. Because of his sensitive nature, the kennel setting, the noise and daily training requirements proved just too stressful for him. He was doing extremely well while in the training areas. However, when returned to the kennel setting, he continued to lose weight and wasn't able to adjust to his surroundings. For health reasons, he was released from the program, and his life-long dream of assistance to others came to an end.

When the folks received the call regarding Kessen's release from the program, they immediately drove to the facility and adopted him. Because he had been ill, he was hardly recognizable except for his black, nickel-shaped patch of fur on his side. Over a period of weeks, the folks nursed him back to health and searched for a program that would meet his need to help others. After working toward a new goal in a different type of program, Kessen qualified as a therapy dog. He and our dad worked as an assisted therapy team in a library program and in school settings with both autistic children and with children in wheel chairs. A dream Kessen thought was gone forever was revived in a different manner.

Kessen was helping others.

Why was Kessen telling me this now? I certainly wasn't fearful of new experiences, but hearing about his stint in Puppy College was a bit intimidating...even for me. Just hearing the word *rigorous* caused my hackles to rise a bit, and my hackles weren't used to working either. My hackles and I apparently shared the same work ethic. Since nothing seemed to really bother me, my hackles were idle for lengthy periods of time.

Kessen was amazed at my relaxed and pensive nature. Perhaps, daily attention to my appearance had a calming effect on me. I also developed an interest in *feng shui* as a means of creating a sense of calm in all situations. When going for walks with the folks, I ignored most of what went on around me. My conduct remained undisturbed while dogs barked, trucks rolled by and children rode past on bikes. Not only was reacting wildly to various types of disturbances considered unproductive, responding loudly might cause wrinkles in my well-groomed appearance. As far as I was concerned, nothing was worth taking that sort of risk.

After thinking about the situation, being concerned about the daunting rigors of Puppy College was just a minor consideration for me. As far as I was concerned, the new and exciting experiences that awaited me held the promise of meeting new dogs and possibly gaining more techniques for grooming and beauty tips. I refused to even think about the perils of rigorous training.

Upon hearing my thoughts about entering Puppy College, Kessen just shook his head and laughed. He knew what difficult situations loomed in my future and wondered just how my beauty regimen would fit into the kennel setting. According to him, I was in for one big surprise as well as a shock to my system. He worried unnecessarily since I could and would handle anything thrown at me. After all, I was a canine fashionista whose presence would undoubtedly brighten up those kennel surroundings.

The day finally came for the family to take me to Puppy College. Kessen assumed his down position in the back, and I was in the portable canvas crate that gave me so much grief as a young puppy. Notice how I blamed the crate

and not my behavior for the misfortune of getting my teeth stuck while shrieking at the top of my lungs in the car? Nevertheless, I was now ready for the journey, and as we left the driveway of the house that became

We were ready for the trip.

my home, a fleeting feeling of sadness passed over me. Seeing the image of my home disappear in the distance was slightly reminiscent of my leaving the house in California. However, this particular sensation was a bit different because I somehow knew that someday I'd return to the sorority house. I don't know why I felt that way...I just did. That feeling of sadness quickly disappeared, and the excitement of encountering new experiences loomed in my future.

The folks were quite sad about my leaving them, but they knew this day was coming. During the week before my leaving, they took me to visit the numerous friends I had made during my year with them and even attempted to take me to a fun-swim at the Natural Healing Center. Did they not know me by now? My paws, let alone my entire body, were not about to get submerged in some over-sized bath tub called a pool. In keeping with my No Wet Clause, I refused to even get near the ramp that led to the pool. While they hoped that I would enjoy the fun-swim experience as much as Kessen did before he went to Puppy College, I was sorry to disappoint them. I was totally devoted to my avoidance of water for the sake of maintaining my flawless appearance.

As we pulled into the circular driveway of the facility, Kessen refused to raise his head due to his Fear of Car Windows Syndrome. He said a muffled goodbye from the back of the car and wished me luck. He didn't even want to look at the facility because of his earlier stressful training experience. I understood his reaction and acknowledged his goodbye as Dad took me from the canvas crate. As I surveyed the campus grounds, they looked fairly nice with multicolored flowers lining the circular driveway. A most colorful sign in the shape of a huge paw print welcomed visitors. This Puppy College campus looked pretty cool!

Last night, Kessen told me that I was not to look back at the folks when they handed my leash to the trainer. That was the canine tradition so as not to make the folks think we were not prepared or going to miss them so much that we'd screw up. They wanted each dog to be successful, and I wasn't going to mess with tradition. So, I walked nicely by the trainer's side and never looked back.

As I entered the facility with the trainer, I was taken aback by the somewhat primitive living conditions. While the kennels were quite spacious, the floors were entirely made of concrete. At the far end of the kennel was a sliding door that opened up to spacious dog run. At least I'll have an opportunity to stretch my legs and do my daily conditioning exercises. Fortunately, my assigned kennel's position was in complete compliance with my belief in *feng shui.* I would need all the help I could get in terms of inner calm in this place.

Metal food and water bowls were available but no sign of a soft bed anywhere on the premises. How disheveled would my sleek coat and tail look after sleeping on concrete? This was not acceptable by any means, and I definitely had to find a way to get some sort of soft bed for sleeping. Judging from the sparse accommodations, my reputation as a fashionista extraordinaire must not have preceded my arrival.

The trainer, oblivious to my dismay over the living conditions, led me to my kennel. I was pleasantly surprised to see that I had a kennelmate. She was a rather large

Labrador Retriever, with a blonde coat like mine and a most impressive well-toned body. Because of my petite size, I appeared a bit dwarfed next to her, but I wasn't at all intimidated. In addition to her size, her expressive eyes were her most striking attribute. Although I thought my eyes were dramatic in shape and color, her eyes were spectacular in terms of brightness and intensity. Her overall appearance and demeanor suggested both self-confidence and sincerity which somehow predicted success in this program, yet she didn't seem affected by her appearance at all. She was definitely one of those dogs Kessen talked about in terms of having unique qualifications for service to others. Bark and howl about irony...the pretentious fashionista shared a kennel with a sincere and gentle soul. Who was in charge of those arrangements? I wished Kessen were here to witness this situation. He'd hoot and howl about it for weeks!

My kennelmate's name was Deonna, and her life-long dream was to be successful as an assistance dog. We

Deonna was the real deal!

both had the same training in terms of commands and public etiquette responsibilities. Yet, she seemed to be quite serious about the program while I was just here to take in the sights and perhaps share some much-needed beauty techniques with the residents. My sharing a few decorating tips wouldn't hurt either. Because I didn't want to reveal my slightly

137

superficial qualities so early in our kennelmate relationship, I didn't share my thoughts regarding assistance with Deonna. We just chatted about our backgrounds and awaited the next step in the program.

We didn't have to wait very long for the trainers to greet us. Both Deonna and I were taken from the kennel area to another room for our temperament tests. The trainers took us through a series of exercises as we demonstrated our proficiency in terms of commands, were handled from the tip of our noses to tails to see if we tolerated that type of treatment and judged in numerous ways before being allowed to continue in the program. Some dogs didn't pass the tests, but we were lucky. Both of us passed the tests and were happy to return to our kennel knowing that we made it through the initial testing process. In spite of my nonchalance over being here, washing out of the program on the first day would have been a real downer let alone a great source of embarrassment.

As I looked around this huge room, dogs of all colors and sizes filled the kennels in the living quarters. Some barked, a few slept, but most were trying, in their own ways, to adjust to the changes in their living situations. After all, we probably all came from a house having a nice family, perhaps enjoyed the company of another friendly dog and appreciated the luxury of sleeping in a soft, comfortable bed at night. This

No luxury accommodations....

lackluster living situation was a drastic change for each of us as well as quite a shock to our systems. That disbelief registered on each of the faces staring out from the chain link of the kennel doors. I'll bet each dog wondered how to adjust to this situation...I know I did, and I wasn't even serious about being here.

Following the evening meal, which consisted of the same food I ate at home minus cooked vegetables, the sliding door at the back of the kennel opened, and I was able to stretch my legs for a while. Deonna and I just sat around while breathing the fresh air and enjoying the glow of the sunset. The dogs in the other kennels seemed to be enjoying the same sights. Perhaps the enjoyment of these moments was the sign each of us needed that gave us hope for the next day to be better than this one. Truth be told, it was comforting to believe in that notion.

When all of the dogs returned to their respective kennels, the bright lights were dimmed for the night giving the kennel area a most ominous look. Dogs moving around in their kennels in the dim lighting cast shadows on the walls creating unsettling silhouettes. If I thought the kennel area looked gloomy in the daylight, it looked like a ghost town at night.

I'll admit that I was intimidated by everything that was happening and wondered how I might find some common ground...something that reminded me of home that would boost my spirits and take away the creepy thoughts about the kennels. Looking over at Deonna, who chose a corner of the kennel as her bed for the night, I saw a look of total contentment in her face as she slept. How in the world of treats and toys was that dog able to sleep so soundly in this place? Dogs were barking, howling at an imaginary moon, whining and snoring. In my opinion, the sounds were ear-shattering, yet Deonna slept soundly. She was definitely in her element while sequestered in this cave-like atmosphere. Judging from the expression of serenity on her face, she probably reveled in the Spartan-like quality of the setting. My mind wandered as I imagined her being a devoted pet for a pioneer family, obediently following their wagons across the rugged terrain while protecting them from snakes and rabid animals. That was definitely her calling. Put me in that scenario, and I'd be the dog riding in the wagon while hiding under a blanket!

Nevertheless, I had to stop imagining strange scenarios and concentrate on my situation. Thinking such peculiar thoughts about Deonna demonstrated how quickly one's mind disregarded common sense when under duress. In order to get my mind out of bizarro-land, I had to focus on what I did best, and paying attention to my appearance was just what this puppy needed.

As of right now, my biggest concern was how I might continue my beauty regimen in this concrete setting. I could almost feel my coat getting dull and drab due to lack of brushing, but there were no combs or brushes in sight. I scanned the shelves at the far wall of the kennel area looking for conditioner for my delicate skin, paw wipes to remove debris, dry bath cloths for some personal hygiene and nail clippers for my perfectly manicured nails. Yet, nothing related to beauty care was in sight. Tomorrow, I'd look around for any evidence of beauty products. I hoped that a place as large as this one was stocked with something useful for proper hygiene. But for tonight, I'd just settle into another corner of the kennel and attempt to get a good night's sleep...on concrete no less!

Morning festivities began at an early hour for those of us sequestered in kennels. It was a bit of a shock to my system to be getting up so early, but Deonna was alert, probably had already done some canine version of Tai Chi and was ready for the day's training...even before eating breakfast. That dog was a candidate for Puppy College Dog of the Year!

I, on the other paw, reserved my energy for the training routines after breakfast which, by the way, consisted of dry dog food from a metal bowl. How was I expected to perform at peak level from that culinary extravagance called breakfast and from a metal bowl no less? Where were the elevated food bowls that eased the strain on our necks when eating or drinking? Well, they weren't here! While taking a moment for some deep breaths, I recognized that my cynicism was not going to get me through the day's routine. I needed to regroup, use Deonna's optimistic outlook as incentive for success and just do what I needed to do in order to see what the program had to offer. It was too early in the game to call it quits. I had a lot to offer this program...especially in the area of beauty and fashion tips. Of utmost importance was finding the right approach for sharing my extensive knowledge of canine beauty care. Planning for that endeavor at night would take my mind off that uncomfortable concrete floor used for a bed.

After breakfast, Deonna and I were taken to the training area where we met a number of dogs of our own age. We were all in what might be called basic training, and none of us really knew what was expected of us. We were each assigned a trainer and went our separate ways in the training area. My trainer and I worked on various commands such as walking nicely on a leash and retrieving objects dropped on the floor. I was adequately prepared for walking nicely, but the purpose of retrieving dropped objects proved a bit of a mystery for me.

For example, a toy was thrown on the floor, and I was given the command to Get it. I did exactly what was expected, grabbed the toy from the floor and handed it over to the trainer when I heard the Give command. I was praised for my obedience, but then a number of toys were thrown on the floor. Attempting to be the top dog in the group and demonstrating that I wasn't just another dog with a pretty face, I immediately retrieved one of the toys and proudly brought it to the

Do you want the toy or not?

trainer. She ignored my attempts to put that toy into her hands. Standing in front of her with that toy hanging from my mouth was embarrassing. Did she want it or not? So, I dropped it on the floor and walked away. As soon as the toy hit the floor, I heard the commands of Get/Give. So, I retrieved the toy and gave it to the trainer, but here was my dilemma: Why didn't she take it when I offered it to her just a few seconds ago? These retrieval exercises were getting confusing.

Later, Deonna told me that I was supposed to wait for the trainer to give me a command before I got the toy from the floor. Responding to commands was the law of the land, and nothing more or less than that principle was tolerated. Apparently, free thinking was an undesirable trait in this training facility. For the very first time, I realized that I was in big, big trouble. I was a color outside-the-dog-house lines kind of gal and not very good with adhering to strict procedures.

Deonna and I talked about the rules and regulations of Puppy College on a daily basis, and she actually found the strict rules of obedience to be comforting. All she had to do was respond to commands and never had to make decisions or think about anything else but being compliant. That philosophy sure didn't fit into my line of thinking, and it didn't take into account time spent on one's appearance.

Where did canine hygiene fit into this training regimen in addition to obedience? Sure, we were taken on outings while wearing ill-fitting capes of less than desirable colors, but what about the care that went into one's appearance before strutting our wares in public? Even though the trainers made sure we had baths before going out in public, which wasn't tops on my agenda, no type of lavender-scented conditioner was used to moisten our coats and fill the air with a scent of mystery and intrigue   That sensory element would have added a level of unsurpassed social status to our training appearances at the nearby mall.

However, my beauty techniques as well as suggestions were totally ignored and lost on this group. All they cared about was learning how to be of assistance to others.

Days turned into weeks and weeks into months as Deonna and I progressed through the training program. We learned new training techniques such as opening doors and drawers with a rope pull. I especially enjoyed opening the refrigerator door because I really had to give that rope a hard tug for it to open. The force of my pulling the rope often made the door bang the wall when opened, but the trainers prepared for that. Each wall had an acrylic plate attached to the wall so the banging door wouldn't damage the wall. Those trainers were pretty smart in terms of anticipating any problems along the way.

Retrieving objects was a bit of a hang-up for me because I wasn't used to doing things like that. In fact, I wasn't used to picking up anything before coming to this training program. However, by the end of the retrieval phase, I was grabbing all sorts of objects from the floor ranging in size from a pencil to a small hammer. Much to the dismay of the trainers, I wasn't doing these exercises willingly. That's when the words *Change of Career* were bantered around the training area.

As the training became more difficult, dogs were released for just being true to their natures. The high-energy dogs, who filled the play areas with excitement as they ran circles around the calmer canines, gradually left the program for either their previous homes or for families waiting to adopt them. Barking, licking, digging, chasing and other typical canine-related behaviors were becoming

144

nonexistent as dogs who exhibited those traits left the kennels. The remaining dogs, myself included, now exhibited extraordinary skills and hardly resembled the group who filled the kennels on the day of our arrival.

Deonna enjoyed and excelled in just about everything that was presented to her. She was even turning lights on

and off from a wall switch. If I didn't know her so well, I'd think she was showing off, but she was determined to learn as much as she could about helping others. I, on the other paw, was finding each day more challenging than the previous one. My struggle wasn't with the training regimen but with

Deonna's incredible!

something considerably more personal. Deonna and I were truly opposites in terms of dedication. I didn't have the same desire to be successful in this program that she had, and I just decided not to hide it anymore. Pretending to enjoy working toward assistance just wasn't working for me any longer.

When in the training area, the trainers were quick to pick up on my nonchalance and change in attitude. My unwillingness to cooperate and respond to basic commands was a giant clue for them. At first, it was thought that I was just having a bad day. As days turned into weeks, the realization that I had mentally and physically checked out from the program became evident. As a result, the paperwork began for my release from the program.

Deonna noticed the changes in my behavior, and we

discussed the situation. I was honest with her in that this program was never meant for me. This assistance gig was her true calling, and her total success with every single training exercise was proof of that vocation. I was the fashion-savvy pretender, and my staying here wasn't fair to the trainers or the well-meaning dogs who were seriously striving for success. Kessen was right when he told me that assistance dogs were very special dogs. Truth be told, I

This career was not meant for me.

didn't have that special something that made those dogs so wonderful. Nevertheless, I had other talents to share and a different path to follow in life. Knowing what path was meant for me just wasn't within my grasp at this moment in time, but I'd find it someday. I had no doubt that I would.

So, I said my goodbye to Deonna, and while she was genuinely sad to see me leave the program, she totally understood my motivation for leaving. She was in her element in this training program, and I had no doubt that she would be successful as an assistance dog. In addition to that vocation, her well-toned body and blonde coat really looked chic in her cape!

When the folks got the dreaded call that I was being released, they rushed out to get me. Because I was in the program for three months and received favorable reports up until the last few weeks, they were genuinely surprised. They wanted to adopt me and hoped I wasn't in the same sickly condition as Kessen was when he was released. After all of the paperwork was signed and my adoption was official, the trainer brought me out to the waiting room. After an enthusiastic greeting, I pranced out of the facility as if I had been at a vacation spa. As far as I was concerned, my campus caper was a thing of the past. This clean, lean manipulating machine was back and ready to rock and roll...

My experience at Puppy College not only gave me additional training but also insight into the strength of character required to be an assistance dog to someone in need. Deonna had that quality, and I was most grateful to have shared a kennel, although concrete, with her.

Years later while at a fund raiser for a canine assisted therapy organization, I happened to spot an elegant, blonde assistance dog walking next to a person in a wheel chair. As the assistance team came closer, I immediately recognized Deonna. When they came even closer to my booth, she also recognized me. So as not to deviate from her role as silent guardian, Deonna gave me a nod of recognition. Those spectacular eyes of hers said it all...this role of assistance was her destiny, and she was enjoying every minute of it. Way to go, Deonna!

12

Paws with a Cause

I was now an official Change of Career dog. Did that title upset me in any way? Not a chance! The freedom I felt while walking out of the training facility with my mom was exhilarating. I can't say that I tried my best at the assistance gig because I never really did. That truth would be disappointing to Kessen if I decided to tell him, but I wasn't making any hasty decisions regarding true confessions based upon my newly acquired freedom. I'd wait until we were together for a while before I played the honesty card.

No true confessions today!

The time spent at Puppy College wasn't an entire waste of time. I learned training techniques involving retrieval methods which quite possibly would never be used by me ever again. Surprise of all surprises, I reached a higher level of leash behavior by walking nicely on a flat collar. While I don't think it's wise to share the techniques the trainer used to achieve that goal, let's just say I was a quick learner!

I also made a number of friends while sequestered in the kennels and had the distinct honor of being Deonna's kennelmate. She, being such a special dog, was definitely going to go far in terms of assistance. That gal was destined for success and how unusual for us to be paired together. If ever there were an odd couple, we were definitely it!

My only regret is that I was unable to share my expertise in the areas of beauty and fashion with the residents of the kennels. Those special dogs, who were moving forward in the program toward a career in assistance, certainly didn't focus on appearance. While they had a natural beauty about themselves due to their willingness to serve others, a little help in the coat-care, moisturizer and mani-pawdi areas wouldn't have hurt. But, that's only my fashionista's opinion and probably not well-acknowledged on the canine runway toward assistance. Now, I just had to face Kessen who was probably huddling in the back seat of the car in his *fear of car windows* position.

My thoughts about Kessen weren't far from the truth. While waiting for my adoption paperwork to be completed, my mom told me that Kessen had quite a difficult time when they reached the driveway of the facility. His memory of the stressful time in this environment overcame him, and he was in a bit of a frenzy. Dad was able to get him to relax, but by now, Kessen was probably huddled in the back seat of the car. He didn't know that during the last few days of my incarceration at the facility, I devised a plan for assisting him with his fear of car windows. I knew that he'd be in the car when the folks came to pick me up, so it was the perfect setting to test my powers of persuasion in the fear department. He was always there to help me, and now it was my turn to help him through this issue.

When we reached the car, I was surprised that I wasn't led to the back of the car where my crate was located. I was shocked to learn that since I was now a member of the family, my car-riding position was in the back seat of the car with Kessen. This Change of Career status definitely had its perks!

I jumped into the back seat to find Kessen crouched near the opposite door. I believed he was happy to see me but couldn't tell from his huddled position on the seat. Seeing his ears wiggle a bit assured me of that fact. While I assumed a compliant position, my mom had a special treat for me...my very own car harness. Believe it or not, it was fashion-forward with its jet-black color, faint outline of red on the trim and soft sheepskin lining. This harness was suitable for all occasions and was the equivalent of a woman's little black dress! I was now thoroughly engrossed in my fashion fantasy which included looking glamorous and impeccably dressed while riding in a car. What dog could ask for more?

As the car started down the driveway, I returned my focus to Kessen and my plan for assisting him. I had to be slick about this endeavor because Kessen was quite smart and would recognize a ruse very quickly. So, I chatted aimlessly about some of my experiences in an animated fashion for a while and then suddenly became completely silent. My abrupt silence caused Kessen to take notice, and he inquired as to my well-being. I remained silent as he continued to question me. Finally, I told him that I wasn't sure what was happening to me, but I was experiencing a strong sense of nervousness and panic. I wasn't sure what to do since I felt frozen in place and unable to move one way or another.

At first Kessen thought I might be playing a trick on him. However, he became concerned when I began to shiver and believed that I was, indeed, experiencing some sort of delayed reaction to the campus experience. He attempted to soothe me from his huddled position on the car seat with a calming tone of voice, but that tactic had no effect on my condition. In order to help me, he had to sit up and help me through the anxiety.

He faced his fears for me.

Even knowing that sitting up would cause nausea on his part due to his fears, he just took a deep breath and sat up to face me. While queasiness took over, Kessen fought back the feeling because he was my big brother and had to help. Taking some deep breaths momentarily eased the dizziness, and he was able to sit up calmly and talk to me about my situation. He avoided looking at the passing scenery and instead concentrated on me and my shaky condition. He snuggled close to me in the hopes of lending some brotherly support and assistance. He spoke in soothing tones and hoped that my lapse into this most unusual panic mode might subside. Looking deeply into my eyes for some sign of recovery or clue for some way to help, he saw a slight flicker of amusement in my almond-shaped eyes and immediately knew he had been duped by my actions.

Kessen was furious that I had both frightened and fooled him. He now wanted nothing to do with any explanations on my part, and not even fluttering my long eyelashes softened his anger. In the past, that feminine technique usually worked its magic. Nevertheless, while acting all pompous and indignant about the situation, he never noticed that he was sitting upright and looking calmly out of the car windows for the very first time in his life. If not for my devious plot, he'd be huddled on the seat of the car staring at the door handle. I knew he'd come around eventually and forgive me. Everything worthwhile takes time, and how could he possibly resist my feminine charms? No dog has ever been able to do that!

Midway on the drive home, Kessen did have a bit of a twinkle in his eye as he watched the scenery from an upright sitting position in the car. I had told him many months ago that there would come a time when I would help him through some serious situation. At the time, he just laughed at the absurdity of my prediction, but that day came without warning for him. As he remembered that prophesy of mine, he just smiled, and without any exchange of words, I knew we were good to go and ready to move forward not just as members of a pack but as a family. My well-manicured paws definitely worked for a worthwhile cause today.

As the car pulled into the driveway of the house that was now my permanent home, Kessen looked me straight in the eyes and apologized for not being with me when the inevitable event happened. I wasn't sure what event he was talking about until we entered the house. As I always did when coming or going, I checked my appearance in the glass of the patio door and was immediately shocked at what I saw. Sometime while incarcerated in that training facility, the middle of my beautiful, black nose had turned a pale shade of mauve. How and when

OMG!

did that happen? Since I saw no mirrors or glass doors in the training facility, I never had the opportunity to view my appearance. I just took it for granted that I looked totally marvelous. That change had to be the result of the stagnant air in the kennels. What must Deonna think of me now? Perhaps she thought it was a new fashion-forward look since mauve was an elevated shade of pink. I suppose one could always hope since my reputation as a fashionista was at stake.

Too funny!

Although Kessen's concern for my frenzy over the change in the color of my nose seemed fairly sincere, his telling me about it made me wonder a bit about his motives. He knew what pride I had in my regal, black nose and probably recalled how, as a young puppy, I once guaranteed my nose would never change colors. At the time, I also

154

made fun of his pink nose. In hindsight, that conversation wasn't one of my finer moments.

While Kessen apologized for having to tell me about my nose condition, I knew he was inwardly chuckling about it. After thanking me once again for assisting him through his serious fear issue, Kessen, in his unsurpassed wisdom as pack leader, reminded me that in life, no good deed goes unpunished. He sure had a way with words, and his telling me about my nose changing colors after I helped him with his fear issue was definitely proof of that fact...

The day I left Puppy College for my Change of Career status was the beginning of so many amazing events in my life. The first and foremost was the beginning of a great and lasting friendship with Kessen. Our relationship started out with Kessen being the leader of the pack, and I was the reluctant, in-house trainee. With each passing year, our relationship grew and became what we both considered the friendship of a lifetime. A relationship like that doesn't come along often, and I thank my lucky treats that Kessen chose me, in spite of my idiosyncrasies, to be his life-long friend.

155

Work Ethic

There is a term that is as foreign to me as polyester is to being an acceptable fabric on a dog's bed. That term is *work ethic* and totally contradicts everything that makes me the delightful diva that I am. Even using the words individually causes laughter from those who know me.

Kessen will attest to the fact that I rarely work. When I do, it's under extreme pressure from the folks. If I could avoid it, I'd have as little to do with working as possible. In terms of ethics, I do stretch the bounds of most acceptable principles. Having ethics would not be one of the first descriptive words used regarding my character. That doesn't make me a bad dog...just a dog who might stretch boundaries a bit for personal gain and who accepts very few responsibilities.

Unfortunately, upon my return from Puppy College, the folks didn't read my discharge papers. I was a Change of Career dog based upon the premise that I wasn't doing the work in training for assistance. What was different now? I didn't work before I went to Puppy College...didn't do the required work while in Puppy College and was now expected to change my ways and work?

Well, I'll tell you the actual difference...it is my understanding that I went from a concrete kennel to a softer version of captivity involving work. Kessen was in his glory over this predicament of mine and actually rolled around the floor with glee over the situation. I thought it was most unprofessional as well as unattractive for the leader of the pack to act in such a manner.

When did this ridiculous proposal regarding my working become a possibility? Well, it all started when I left Puppy College and was having no residual side-effects from the experience. I was so happy to be home that I found a comfortable spot on my special dog bed that was still in its

This is what I call living the good life!

original place and just snuggled in for a good rest. I slept like there was no tomorrow in my comfortable, orthopedic bed with not even a second thought about my months in concrete captivity. Physically, my skeletal structure took a few hits on that concrete and will probably need some recovery time from that kennel experience, but I'm still rather flexible and open to new and adventurous experiences. I was good to go!

Nevertheless, Kessen warned me that the folks had a strict rule about having no *couch potatoes* in their house. What did that even mean? To begin with, I wasn't allowed on the couch in the first place, but would I be able to jump onto the couch as long as I didn't carry a potato? That *couch potato* issue just didn't make sense. Why would I even want to bring a potato on the couch, and how would I even get it from the vegetable bin?

I must have missed a great deal of important information while in Puppy College because I just wasn't connecting with the program here at home. Maybe my mind was on some sort of delayed processing from the college experience. Because it was just too confusing, I went back to sleep...a very deep sleep that didn't require one bit of work on my part.

Kessen explained everything to me the next day. Being a *couch potato* referred to a dog who did nothing but lay on the couch all day long and sleep. Now, I understood the couch reference, but what did the potato have to do with anything? Kessen ignored my potato inquiry and just told me that I wasn't about to spend my days lounging around the house while attempting new grooming techniques.

As a way to avoid my being a *couch potato*, the folks were going to find a suitable job for me. A job? Doesn't evidence pointing to my not having a work ethic have any credibility in terms of their plan? I just got home from what some might consider a harrowing experience and was now expected to put it all behind me and go to work? I'll admit that description of my stay at Puppy College was rather dramatic because I actually found the experience quite interesting...except for the concrete kennel part. However, I certainly wasn't going to share that information with Kessen. If I played the dreadfully frazzled dog, they might give me the same consideration they gave Kessen when he returned.

Kessen was ill for six weeks following his return from Puppy College and was pampered every day. When he finally recuperated from his traumatic experience, the folks enrolled him in a program for canine assisted therapy. They knew he wanted to help others, and being a therapy dog was the perfect answer to his dream. After weeks of training for the new program, Kessen and our dad became a team to work in programs that helped others. Kessen was in his glory, and Dad loved being Kessen's team partner. They worked in a school program with children in wheel chairs as well as a classroom of children with autism. The children played canine assisted games, walked Kessen in the halls with the help of a specially-made double leash, brushed him and gave him treats of green beans from a plastic fork. Kessen loved getting beans from the children, and they loved giving them to him in that manner because his whiskers didn't tickle their hands when he took the treat. Kessen also was involved in a library Reading with Rover program where children read to the dogs. He loved this program and had his own following of children who couldn't wait to read to him. Kessen was in his element and enjoying every moment of it.

That was Kessen's experience, but now I had to figure out what my next move would be in order to get some pampering of my own. I might just mope around a little, show some disinterest in the meals and walk instead of run

I need pampering...not a job.

to the yard in the hopes that the folks might pick up on my pitiful demeanor. Because I had quite a flair for the dramatic, playing the troubled, young puppy recovering from concrete incarceration was certainly worth the effort and, might I add, I was doing it well!

Kessen knew that I was planning something to get myself out of the compulsory work situation and called me aside for one of his Leader of the Pack talks. He saw right through my intentions and warned me that his wrath would come down hard on me if I attempted to fool the folks. He was adamant about my having to face facts, go to work and above all, learn to enjoy it! Who was he kidding?

Now, there was no way of getting around the inevitable. Kessen was the pack leader, and following his command was essential to my well-being here at home. I was just short of getting the *stink eye* from him, and his giving that to me was his last resort for non-compliance from a subordinate in the pack. I was only on the long-distance receiving line of the *stink eye* once as a puppy, and thought that his method of submission would bore a hole in my head.

It happened when I was running around with Milani at the barbecue in South Carolina. She and I were giving multiple haircuts to the day lilies that lined the fence. After we had completed our hair-care adventure, Milani and I found a comfortable place in the grass to rest. After resting

Kessen was giving me the stink eye!

a bit, I happened to look across the huge yard to where the older dogs were playing. Suddenly, I saw Kessen staring at me with the intensity of a heat–seeking missile...one that was directed exclusively toward me. Evidently, he had witnessed my mass destruction of the plants and wasn't at all pleased.

We were guests in this yard, and I had tarnished that invitation by my haircutting mischief. His eyes seemed to glow as his stare extended across the length of the yard. How was he able to do that? Nevertheless, I was paralyzed with fear...this had to be the *stink eye* that I was warned about by our neighbor dog named Sammy. According to Sammy, I was to avoid that consequence at all costs. Now, I knew what he meant by his warning.

After seeing the long-distance version of the *stink eye* from across the yard, I attempted an apologetic look and hoped that Kessen accepted my apology. Apparently, he did because he turned his steely stare from my direction and walked away to join the other dogs. I was safe for the moment but would remember this incident for a very long time.

Remembering that day lily haircutting incident and subsequent clash with the long-distance *stink eye* now brought back the terror of the moment. It was rumored that Kessen could stare directly into a puppy's eyes and, if he wanted to, might momentarily take away sight or bore a hole in a puppy's head. That was the chilling rumor that floated around the neighborhood, and I believed it. He could be one scary dude when pushed to his limits, and my insistence on work-avoidance was bringing him closer to crossing that boundary line. I certainly didn't want a repeat of that earlier puppy experience. So, in an effort to save myself from the dreaded *stink eye* and possible loss of sight or hole in my head, it was my turn to go to work. Believe me, a working lifestyle wasn't something I had planned for my future.

Within weeks of my return, the folks enrolled me in the identical program that trained Kessen, and after a few weeks of training, I also qualified as a canine assisted therapy dog. Truth be told, I enjoyed the training sessions. I met other dogs, and some even felt the same way about working as I did. In addition to a comprehensive review of basic obedience, I learned to jump through a hula hoop,

I was dressed for success!

play a bowling game for dogs and made Kessen and the folks proud by learning to play a toy piano. I saw myself as being a real hit on the lounge circuit, but unfortunately, that job wasn't offered in animal assisted therapy. On the plus side of this working endeavor, I was given a most fashionable cape to wear while working in a program. The cape's color was a vibrant shade of red that had black trim and a rainbow patch signifying the organization. The entire ensemble contrasted nicely with my blonde coat and truly accentuated my slender figure. I exemplified couture of the highest canine level. If I had to work, at least I was well-dressed and runway-ready!

After my successful completion of training, Mom visited various programs to determine what might be best for me. She thought it might be beneficial for me to begin therapy work as a member of a team with Kessen. He would be a mentor for me as I began my world of work.

Welcome to the world of work!

We began our animal assisted therapy work in the library's Reading with Rover program. Children signed up to read for fifteen-minute intervals to dogs on Saturday mornings. There were four dogs to a Saturday session, and each had a place in a corner of the room. Blankets were put on the floor for the children to sit on while reading to the dog of their choice. The handlers were only there to hold the leashes, and the children dealt only with the dogs. It was an interesting concept, and the children really enjoyed their time with the dogs. While books were available to the children, most brought their own books and settled comfortably next to the dog of their choice. Kessen had his very own following, and children rushed to read to him.

I enjoyed the program immensely, but it did have a bit of a down side for me. I was never a *morning dog* and rarely opened my eyes until around noon. This program began at 10 a.m., so I was not necessarily at my best. Sometimes, I tended to close my eyes while a child read to me which was really rude on my part, but I couldn't help myself. Mom, noticing this tendency and realizing that I was just being me, placed the toe of her shoe under my stomach as I positioned myself on the blanket next to the child. If she saw my eyes fluttering a bit or my head beginning to bob, she'd flex her toe, and that motion kept me awake. After a few weeks, I was used to the early morning schedule, and Mom didn't have to use her toe-prod to keep me awake anymore.

While Kessen and I shared time in the Reading with Rover program at the library, which is where I met my very first love named Rufus, I also volunteered in additional programs. I spent time in the adolescent detention center and worked with a group of boys who were learning dog obedience training and everyday care for dogs. It was in that facility that I had a most disturbing experience. While working on obedience commands, a group of chairs that had been stacked unexpectedly fell to the floor. The sound of those chairs hitting the floor was like an explosion in my ears. I slipped on the shiny surface of the gym's floor and landed on my hip. The pain was excruciating for a few minutes but subsided after resting a bit. I was finally able to walk but unexpectedly had an unusual fear of the shiny floor that caused me to slip. I was frozen with fear about hurting myself again. After my mom's many attempts to get me to leave the gymnasium, I finally conjured up the courage to leave the building. However, I vowed never to walk on a shiny floor again. While my thinking was pretty illogical, the thought of shiny floors being dangerous was very real to me.

My fear of shiny floors raised an additional problem since I also worked in the Pediatric Oncology Waiting Room at the hospital, and most of the floors leading to the waiting room were shiny. The folks weren't sure what to do, but Kessen came to the rescue.

For the next three weeks, Kessen walked in front of me while giving me the courage to trust and follow him through the maze of shiny floors. We didn't get far during the first few days, but every day after that, we got farther and farther along the maze of shiny hospital floors. Eventually, we traveled together to the Pediatric Oncology Waiting Room where I realized that I could now get there on my own due to his assistance. Kessen was always there to help me through difficult times. He was much more than a big brother...he was my devoted friend.

Now that I could bravely walk on the shiny floors to the Pediatric Oncology Waiting Room without Kessen's encouragement, I spent special time with young children in the waiting room. It was in that particular setting that I realized how fortunate I was in terms of my health. These brave children took me for short walks in the carpeted hallway, put countless stickers on my body and played endless brain games with me while they waited for test results. I learned so much from them and would forever be grateful for their enjoyment of my visits. For the first time in my life, I felt humbled to be in their presence. Having that feeling was new to me and didn't sound like me at all!

I never thought helping others just by being there for them was an option. Why didn't someone tell me earlier that it was so easy to help others? I became so involved in my volunteering that it even surprised Kessen. But, we had other obligations coming our way. Another puppy was probably coming to the house, and our responsibility was to assist with the socialization of that newcomer.

Small wire kennels were now situated in various corners of the house, and a gate was put up between the kitchen and the hallway. I remembered that gate from my first encounter with Kessen many months ago. At the time, that gate look huge from my puppy vantage, but now it just looked like a typical gate. I suppose it was meant to intimidate a smaller pup, and from my own experience, it certainly did its job. Of course, Kessen looking like a giant dog didn't help either. Smaller food bowls were next to the main kitchen kennel, and a box filled with small, squeaky toys was placed next to the kennel.

There definitely was a new puppy coming, and for me, it was an exciting time. I was now second in command of the pack and was responsible for assisting with mentoring this new arrival. Kessen and I would work together as a team. He would be the enforcer of the house rules since he was leader of the pack. My job involved teaching puppy etiquette that included respect for the leader of the pack, appropriate puppy-bowl

Mentoring a puppy was going to be fun!

manners when eating and drinking, toy appreciation, yard behavior as well as proper attitudes toward grooming. Puppies were notoriously messy because of their young age, and it was essential to guide them from the very beginning of their training. I was primed and ready for my first assignment as a mentor.

Kessen and I were ready to approach the training of this new puppy as a team. It was a new adventure for both of us, but we were up to the challenge. We weren't sure how we'd manage, but my new philosophy was that anything worth doing was worth doing well. Where did that responsible thinking come from, and what happened to the superficial, delightful diva totally involved in appearances and fashion?

I was still that delightful diva, but discovered that I was more than just a pretty face. My beauty and fashionista flair combined with a recently acquired work ethic gave me opportunities for new challenges and adventures. I was just waiting for the right time to strut my stuff on the runway of life. Too dramatic? Just being me...

It took me a while to discover the importance of having a work ethic. Being so involved with my appearance didn't give me much leeway in terms of knowing there were additional ways to make a difference in life. The animal assisted therapy programs that the folks found for me gave me the incentive to willingly give to others without sacrificing my love of fashion as well as a means of discovering my musical talent. I played a mean toy piano in my time working with therapy groups...I was undeniably not just a pretty face

14

Team Training

The new puppy was arriving in a few hours, and I'll admit that I was a bit apprehensive about the entire endeavor. Barking and howling about how Kessen and I will accomplish so much together as a team sounded well and good when we didn't have a puppy in front of us. However, we'd soon have some little tyke staring up at us with huge eyes and great expectations for the future. That was quite an awesome responsibility on our parts and not one to be taken lightly. Judging from past experience, my record in the responsibility department left a lot to be desired.

When we heard the crunch of the car's tires on the snow in the driveway, we knew the folks were home with the puppy. We waited excitedly at the back door. Pack protocol was followed with Kessen in front, and my position was slightly behind him. According to formal protocol, I should have been directly behind him, but I was eager to get a look at the puppy as well.

Marnie

It seemed like an eternity before the door finally opened. When it did, in walked the cutest, black Labrador Retriever puppy to ever cross the threshold of the house. While her coal-black coat was visibly soft and luxurious, her expressive eyes were her most noticeable trait. She was incredibly gorgeous, and her name was Marnie. Since every puppy coming for training was the recipient of a nickname, she was immediately dubbed Marnie Google with the Goo-Goo Googliest Eyes!

While not at all frightened of Kessen, who loomed as large as a giant in front of her, she maintained a respectful distance and sat nicely while waiting to greet us. Judging from this pup's prior training, our job as mentors was going to be a successful walk in the dog park. This little lady had built in manners and was a training dog's dream come true.

All three of us joined in the greeting ritual of sniffing from tip to tail, and Marnie didn't seem the least bit intimidated by the process. After all, Kessen was a giant compared to her as well as leader of the pack. While I was second in command, I was, however, the glamorous one. I certainly posed no threat to her since she could probably tell that I represented the more polished aspect of the pack.

Then, Marnie did something that really surprised us...in the midst of Kessen's greeting, she actually deferred to Kessen's leadership by rolling on her back in submission. She was either extremely polite or attempting to win points with the pack leader. Kessen was in his glory since he was actually getting the respect his position deserved. When he mentioned the respect aspect, he looked directly at me in an accusatory fashion. I felt his look was a bit harsh since I was respectful in different but significant ways. My approach to respect was more of an indirect method rather than overt fawning over the leader. While I was a subordinate member of the pack, I had my image to protect and was not at all inclined to groveling. Marnie, on the other paw, was working her way towards winning the Leader's Pet Award in the pack. If she kept it up, she'd be second in importance to his cherished, yet smelly ring toy.

But, that little tyke was no threat to me. I had a treat bag full of information for that little one, and in time, she'd

realize how beneficial it would be for her to pay attention to me as well. After all, that luxurious coat of hers would soon be in need of conditioner and brushing. She'll need something to offset her puppy appearance when she starts to lose her baby teeth, and she couldn't go to Kessen for that type of assistance. Without my help, all she'd have left

Marnie will need my feminine perspective.

would be those glorious eyes and puppy breath. She'll always have those incredible eyes, but once that puppy breath is gone, people will think of her as just another dog.

By the way, what is so captivating about the scent of puppy breath to humans? I never understood the value of that attraction since good breath in dogs is a sign of a healthy lifestyle that encompasses proper grooming habits. Puppy breath should never take precedence over health and grooming, yet strangely, it's favored in the human world of peculiarities. I find the general principle similar to dogs sniffing each other's butts. That custom is thoroughly acceptable and encouraged in the dog world, yet humans find it an unusually odd behavior. So, humans enjoying puppy breath and dogs involved in sniffing butts are just acceptable oddities when the canine and human worlds collide.

I didn't realize that mentoring this puppy would involve so much philosophy. Perhaps I should just take Marnie's actions for what they were...she was either a possible Leader's Pet Wannabe or just a well-mannered pup. It was early in the game, and I had twelve months to figure it all out.

Kessen and I worked well as a team with Marnie. He handled the pack order protocol, and I was in charge of appropriate indoor and outdoor behavior such as no running or jumping in the house, no jumping on the furniture and no barking at the neighbor dogs when in the yard. I also covered no stealing of toys from other pack members as well as never touching, at all costs, Kessen's cherished ring toy. If that particular rule were to be disregarded, the full force of Kessen's *stink eye* would befall the puppy. Marnie seemed to understand that particular rule more than the others and never once went near Kessen's smelly ring toy.

In our free time, Marnie and I enjoyed a good game of jaw sparring and air snapping. While it sounded threatening, it was just a game and never escalated to anything physical. However, Kessen sometimes could not stand the commotion, the bickering and the noise. He'd step in between us to stop the action. But, as soon as Kessen would leave the area, we'd start all over again.

One day in particular, he was really frustrated with

our noise making. Being a bit sexist, he attributed the noise to our being females and stated that our house should be correctly re-named the sorority house instead of just calling it the house. According to Kessen, additional male dogs were needed, and our high-pitched racket was gradually driving him to guzzle his water

These females are much too noisy!

instead of just drinking it. He also claimed the nonstop noise and agitation was extremely bad for his digestion!

Marnie and I heartily agreed that renaming the house the sorority house was the best idea and how amazing that Kessen thought of it. Before Kessen could recover from this form of logic, the house was officially re-named. We were all just so excited by the new name and hoped many more females would cross the threshold for training. Kessen just shook his head and put his paws over his ears in despair.

After the commotion of the house's name change set in, my responsibilities were discussed in detail. I was in charge of the professional appearance aspects as well as personal hygiene habits of Marnie's training. Under my guidance, Marnie learned that she had designated food and water bowls which were hers and hers alone. That meant all other bowls of food and water on the premises were off limits. She focused on drinking water without drooling all over the floor, practiced how to avoid getting her paws wet by jumping past puddles instead of jumping into them and valued toys as gifts and not something to shred to pieces. Marnie readily excelled and accepted most of my suggestions but did fall short of one important aspect of her training...proper eating habits.

As special as Marnie was in terms of professional and grooming aspects, she was a food glutton. She inhaled her food faster than the speed of a tick jumping from one unprotected dog to another. At each meal, the pup ate like she hadn't been fed in weeks. I don't know how many times I reminded her to take small bites and chew each bit of food slowly, but nothing worked. Marnie continued to swallow food in one, huge gulp.

Kessen was quick to mention my inability to get Marnie to eat in a professional manner. But, in my defense, I was totally lost in terms of stopping her gluttonous and unsightly behavior. Mom, observing my frustration, took over and began hand feeding Marnie. Day after day, little pieces of kibble were swallowed up from Mom's hand, and yet, nothing changed in terms of Marnie's inhalation techniques. Then, Mom decided to put small handfuls of food in her bowl a little bit at a time. That didn't help either because Marnie only learned to inhale faster in order to get to the next handful of food. The next technique involved putting a silver ball into the food bowl causing Marnie to push the ball around to get to her food. Marnie, being Marnie, had other ideas. She grabbed that ball, tossed it out of her bowl and ate like there was no tomorrow.

In defeat, Mom just looked at Marnie and decided that the War of the Food Glutton was lost and, in the grand scheme of things, wasn't a battle she needed to win for

Marnie to qualify for service. Marnie could eat in that insatiable manner without any consequences, so it was best to just move on to other significant issues. I wished I had thought of that justification for losing the battle in the first place. I definitely had a lot to learn in the mentoring department.

All in all, Marnie proved to be a wonderful puppy in training for service. What was interesting was that she

It's laundry day!

seemed to enjoy being with people more than with other dogs. Marnie repeatedly gave up fun time with us in the yard to sit beside our mom as she read the paper in her favorite lounge chair. Housekeeping chores such as assisting with the laundry, organizing cabinets and rearranging throw rugs in the hall were her specialties. If Marnie were able to move furniture, I'm sure she would have rearranged all of the furniture in the entire house. She was just unbelievable in terms of relating to daily household responsibilities.

Marnie loved housework.

Our Marnie was also extremely good in public. She wore her cape proudly and represented the service organization in a most favorable way. We never had any doubts that she would be successful, but she did have a bit of a mischievous side to her.

177

Marnie was getting ready to leave for Puppy College in a few weeks and was sharing her last Christmas with us. Mom and Dad always took a group photo of us, and it was always a special day in our lives. This year, however, Marnie had something special in store for us. We were aptly dressed in Christmas garb while Mom placed us in the appropriate order for the picture. Marnie was situated in the middle while Dad held the treats to hold our attention. I was hoping for bits of dried liver!

Marnie waited for just the right moment to make her move. Just as Mom was about to take the picture, Marnie grabbed Kessen's collar. I, in turn, grabbed Marnie's. Chaos ensued as all three of us ran around the room while Mom and Dad attempted to restore order. While in position again due to the serious look given to us from our mom, the picture was about to be taken. This time, Marnie grabbed my collar, while Kessen, in turn, gripped Marnie's. Once again, we ran around the room in an excited frenzy. This game was a lot of fun!

By this time, Mom had lost her patience because of our mischievous behavior. She repositioned us with Marnie in front of Kessen and put me behind Kessen. No foolishness would come from that arrangement. As usual, Mom was correct in her placement of us, and the photo was successfully taken. Marnie's impish behavior was a bit unusual for her because she was always so good, but both Kessen and I loved it. Her playful side proved that she was a real dog's dog and truly represented the Labrador Retriever breed in keeping with mischief and mayhem. We

dubbed her actions regarding the Christmas photo as the
Tradition of Turmoil and,
in her honor, recreated it to
some extent each year with
puppies in training when
the Christmas photo was
scheduled. Were the kind
folks impressed with that
great tradition? Not totally,

Tradition of Turmoil

but in a small way, I do believe they honestly looked
forward to a repetition in some form in honor of Marnie.

Marnie left us for Puppy College a few weeks later.
Kessen kept watch for her at the front door, and I waited
near the back door of the house for a week or two. I think

Will she come back today?

we knew that she wasn't
coming back to us. Months
later, we heard that Marnie
had been partnered with a
young girl in a wheel chair
and was assisting her in
special ways. We hoped that
Marnie didn't carry on her
Tradition of Turmoil with her
new partner. Yikes!

A few months after Marnie
left us, small kennels were placed in various corners of the
house, lowered food and water bowls were set out, and a
new toy box, complete with small, squeaky toys, was placed
in a prominent position next to the kennel in the kitchen.
Another puppy was coming to the household, and it was our

job to take over the socialization techniques that we perfected with Marnie's training.

Our team training was so successful with Marnie that we thought we'd take our working relationship to a higher level…make it a more professional arrangement. With that in mind, we formed the Socialization Squad. Initially, Kessen wanted to be first in command, but I thought we

Our partnership was now official.

should be equal partners in this endeavor. Since he would always be the pack leader and first in that special position, he relented in terms of our partnership in the Socialization Squad. In an official capacity as squad leaders, we would share responsibilities and work with the puppies who came to the house for training. Marnie's accomplishment in terms of service due to our team training was proof that our newly formed Socialization Squad was destined for success with any pup who crossed the threshold of our house. If we did it with Marnie, we could do it with any pup. In all honesty, we really believed what we were saying!

Those words would reverberate in our heads numerous times over the years starting with the next puppy who taught us that overconfidence is a dangerous attitude when mentoring. With all of our ideas and tactics, we failed to take into account one important detail: Not every pup was like Marnie...

Kessen and I were so excited about our working together in the Socialization Squad. Being a part of the Squad gave me a taste of what it was like to be in charge and have responsibilities of my own. While I never thought of myself as actually having responsibilities, working side by side with Kessen allowed me to follow in Kessen's paw prints for a while and gain insight into the responsibilities of a pack leader. It wasn't until years later that I found out that his giving me certain responsibilities was preparation for the big plans he had with regard to my position in the pack. Kessen always had a plan and being prepared was one of the qualities that made him a great pack leader.

15

Puppies Galore

Over the next ten years, puppies seemed to pass through the house in turnstile-like fashion, and out of necessity, the Socialization Squad went through a number of changes during that time period. We found that each puppy was very different in terms of behavior and required a wide variety of techniques for successful mentoring.

Kessen and I were very naive upon the arrival of the first dog after Marnie's stay with us. We had the ridiculous notion that not only was every dog as easy to train as Marnie was, but also that we were somewhat of an invincible team capable of conquering any and all types of misbehavior in a puppy. It didn't take long before we found out that puppy mentoring was a real job having valid issues and serious responsibilities.

Turin

While we waited for this new puppy, Kessen recalled a story about the first puppy who came to the sorority house before him. The pup's name was Turin, and he came from California just as Kessen and I did. Sammy, the Golden Retriever who lived next door, often spoke of Turin and his daring exploits. Turin was a most unusual puppy, and his exploits led to a legacy that was left unchallenged through the years.

Apparently, Turin had quite the talent for flying through the air. As a puppy, he looked innocent enough, but he was the first and only puppy to jump over the back of the couch. When he was four months old, he managed to frighten the folks speechless by perfecting a flawless SIT in the middle of a glass coffee table. Following that escapade, Turin wasn't able to duplicate that feat because the glass coffee table was gone later in the day.

Turin was a frequent flyer!

According to Kessen's information from Sammy, Turin went on with his daring capers during his free time

but, as he matured, was serious about his training and commitment to helping others. While Turin enjoyed many daring experiences as a young puppy, he went on to a career in service...one that did not include flying through the air.

His flying days were over.

Izzy

Our rapid transit from Turin's story to reality came in the form of a black Labrador Retriever named Izzy. Upon her arrival, she attacked our house with reckless abandon, and nothing was sacred during the chaos. She sped through the house, knocking over an elevated food-bowl stand that caused the falling bowls to shatter on the tile floor, scattered

throw pillows and bounced off doors and walls due to her intense speed. Kessen and I watched her fly by as she circled the room for the second time without any indication of

We're safe here.

slowing down. Such incredible speed and endurance in such a small puppy left us wavering between amazement and apprehension. For safety's sake, we sought refuge from her rampage on the couch.

Bouncing off the china cabinet in the dining room seemed to slow her down, and once recovered, Izzy immediately fell asleep from total exhaustion. When we were convinced of her being asleep, we moved closer to the dining room to get a good look at her. She looked quite innocent while asleep, but we knew what strength and endurance was contained in that little body. I had to give the little pup credit...she could really bounce off a wall, door or cabinet and recover quickly. That dexterity was a most extraordinary talent in my book.

Who was this puppy, and was she battery powered? While this pup's assault on the house seemed to go on forever, it really only took her about five minutes to leave a trail of destruction. The folks were stunned into silence as they observed this

The Black Tornado

newcomer's most unusual arrival and realized for the first time that this puppy, who proved herself to be a weapon of mass destruction within minutes of her arrival, would be with the family for at least twelve months. The tranquility of the house was shattered by a twelve-pound puppy whose mayhem closely resembled that of a tornado sweeping through the house. The chaotic actions upon her arrival earned her the first, but not the last, of many nicknames... she was appropriately called the Black Tornado!

After witnessing the most unusual arrival of this new puppy, I mentioned to Kessen that it was imperative that we re-visit the bylaws of the Socialization Squad. If he wanted to be fully in charge, I'd be willing to give up my equal partnership as a means of respect for him as the leader of the pack. Kessen saw through that proposal immediately since he felt this pup was trouble and knew I was undoubtedly a bit frightened of her. He was correct on both counts

Today would be a better day.

but convinced me that we weren't quitters. We just had to come up with some new approaches to her training. We decided to wait until morning and get a clear view of the situation. Everything always looked better in the morning...so they say.

Believe it or not, things did look better the next day. Izzy was most apologetic for her behavior and explained that she had been kenneled for many weeks prior to coming here and overwhelmed when she first entered the house.

She wasn't making excuses for herself but giving a motive for the chaos. We understood her position, and each of us agreed to a fresh start. After all, not everyone has a good first day, and hers didn't even come close!

As it turned out, Izzy was really quite nice but had no intentions of being an assistance dog. Her goal was to be a champion athlete complete with blue ribbons and trophies. Judging from the speed and endurance exhibited during her arrival, she undeniably had the necessary skills. Because the folks had no way of knowing about her career goal, they continued her assistance training on a daily basis. Izzy even mastered the art of refusals in an effort to get the folks to recognize her true talents.

Izzy took refusals to a higher level and demonstrated that technique in just about every location. No place was too sacred for her to demonstrate her skills. She'd stop in the middle of the street, refuse to leave a restaurant and even declined to leave the training facility after a class but had to relent when the instructor began turning off the lights. She tried just about everything for the folks to understand

The Queen of Refusals

what career she chose for herself, and it wasn't assistance.

At first, Kessen wasn't the least bit interested in what he considered Izzy's shallow goal of glory rather than assistance. In fact, he even ignored Izzy for quite some time. Since he was the pack leader and dictated protocol, I wasn't supposed to have anything to do with Izzy either. I felt sorry for her because, in my heart, I felt she was entitled to her dreams, but I had to respect Kessen's wishes. The neighborhood dogs also followed Kessen's rules with one exception: Finnegan

Finnegan held the title of Neighborhood Dog's Dog, and all the females sat a bit straighter, fluffed their coats and fluttered their eyelashes whenever Finnegan was around. Every female wanted to gain favor with him because he was the neighborhood catch. Some of the dogs even drooled in his presence

Finnegan was a real hunk!

which Izzy found to be a ridiculous and unsanitary attempt to win his favor.

Being strong, lean and adventurous, Finnegan had a distinct advantage over the other male dogs in the neighborhood. He'd strut his stuff, race through the yards in search of prey and never break a sweat. That dog was toned and secretly the envy of the male dogs as well.

Finnegan was also *crushing* on Izzy big time, and she, on the other paw, thought he was a pretentious, egotistical fool and a thorn in her paw. He teased her constantly and insisted on calling her Toots. Izzy was not accustomed to such familiarity and especially disliked his nickname for her. However, getting used to Finnegan was much like getting used to a wart on one's paw. One day, accepting him as a friend just happened for no rhyme or reason.

Finnegan enjoyed Izzy's company in spite of Kessen's shunning and never gave spending time with her a second thought. No one told Finnegan what to do or what not to do. He was a strong, confident dog who just liked Izzy.

Izzy eventually found an extra-special place in her heart for Finnegan after he rescued her from a coyote who had entered the yard at night through an opened gate. Izzy was alone in the darkened yard and only able to see the ghoulish green eyes staring back at her from under a shrub. Not knowing what to do since Kessen and I were inside the house, she just froze in place. Finnegan, who was out for an evening stroll, sensed that Izzy was in trouble. With his powerful legs, he jumped the fence and faced off with the coyote. Emitting a menacing growl through barred teeth, Finnegan sent that coyote running for the opened gate. Izzy was so very relieved and thanked Finnegan for his bravery. She did, however, question his jumping over the fence when he could have just entered through the opened gate. Assuming a stately pose, Finnegan told her that saving a damsel in distress necessitated a grand entrance. Izzy just laughed at his silliness, but his bravery that night sealed their friendship. While she still pretended to reject his advances, Izzy secretly looked forward to his visits, and he continued to pursue her with taunts and really enjoyed calling her Toots!

A few weeks later, Kessen was still ignoring Izzy over the issue of her career goals. A way for Izzy to get back into Kessen's good graces came in the form of a visiting puppy named Tansy. Tansy was being raised by another family but needed someone to watch her for a weekend. Our folks were always willing to help but had to travel to the facility in Michigan to get her. They decided to take us along for the ride and Kessen, Izzy and I shared the back seat. Kessen was still ignoring poor Izzy so the temperature in the back-seat area was icy-cool to say the least. When we got to the facility, we were all anxious to see our weekend visitor. Mom went in to get her and, in a few minutes, came out with this black Labrador Retriever who was nestled comfortably in her

Tansy looked so innocent.

arms. Once they were both in the front seat of the car, we greeted the pup with excited sniffs and snorts from the back seat. She looked like a darling pup and was asleep before we even left the driveway of the facility. She would be a quiet weekend visitor...or so we thought. Little Tansy slept all the way home from the facility, and that was the last time she slept!

As it turned out, Tansy was a self-proclaimed good-time girl and a real party-pup. Her goal was to cram as much fun as possible into her weekend with us. Kessen, seeing what a great challenge Tansy might be, offered Izzy the job of puppy sitting for the entire weekend in exchange for possible reconsideration of

Puppy sitting was exhausting!

190

her career goals. Because Izzy had been so lonely due to Kessen's shunning of her, she jumped at the chance to puppy sit for tiny Tansy. How difficult would it be? After all, she was just a puppy!

Energetic Tansy ran Izzy ragged both inside the house and outside in the yard. That adventurous puppy thought of Izzy as a chew toy as well as a mountain to climb on, over, under and around. Kessen and I watched from the sunroom. While I had hoped to intervene, Kessen reminded me that Tansy was Izzy's special responsibility for the weekend. Kessen believed she could and would handle the situation with Tansy…all by herself.

On the second day, Izzy looked considerably haggard from Tansy's care and decided that having Tansy in the yard was better than chasing her all over the house. Walking to the yard, Tansy happened to notice Kessen's prized ring toy hanging from a low-hanging hook. Izzy warned her not to even think of touching it because it would bring the wrath of Kessen down on both of them and perhaps even earn them the *stink eye*. Tansy, pretending to listen to Izzy's warning, walked on by and headed for the yard. As Izzy nonchalantly followed her, knowing the mountain-climbing abuse would begin once in the yard, Tansy suddenly doubled back, grabbed that ring toy and headed for the yard. Izzy was mortified and hoped that Kessen hadn't noticed Tansy's disobedience. However, once in the yard, Izzy saw Kessen and me looking at them through the sunroom windows. There was trouble brewing, and Izzy had to find a way to get that toy from Tansy.

After chasing her around the yard, zig-zagging in and around all of the shrubs and bushes, Izzy was not only exhausted but wasn't sure getting that ring toy was even possible. Tansy was just too fast, and her energy level certainly exceeded Izzy's at that point. She'd never get back into Kessen's good graces if she didn't get that toy back from Tansy.

Stopping to catch her breath and assess the situation, Izzy remembered Linus' Three step Action Plan that Kessen had taught her weeks ago. As Tansy taunted her with the ring toy, Izzy curled her lip, gave a low-sounding growl and a rather muffled snap in Tansy's direction. Those three movements only made Tansy laugh and taunt Izzy even more. As Tansy got closer and closer, Izzy gave up and told her that she had won...she could have Kessen's toy. Tansy, thinking it was true, came even closer to Izzy to deliver a victory howl. Tansy was unaware that Izzy, using her canine ingenuity as well as her fear of Kessen's wrath,

Success!

added another step to Linus' Action Plan. At the instant that Tansy opened her mouth for her victory howl, Izzy grabbed that toy as it dropped from her mouth, ran through the dog run and into the sunroom where she dropped the toy at Kessen's front paws. Izzy sat respectfully in front of him while she waited for some response. Kessen commended her for retrieving his toy as well as adding another step to

Linus' Action Plan. He had quite a laugh about the entire situation and recognized how hard Izzy had worked with her puppy sitting assignment. As a result, Kessen welcomed Izzy back into the pack, and the dogs resumed a peaceful existence in the sorority house.

Tansy, having been out-maneuvered by Izzy, was a compliant visitor for the remainder of the weekend. Once Tansy left, Izzy breathed a huge sigh of relief. She was back in the pack once again and regarded as a responsible member of the family. If only Kessen would accept her dream of athletic glory as being something worthwhile as a career. That acknowledgement on his part would make the weekend a total success.

Within a week or two, Kessen saw how dedicated Izzy was to her dream and relented. Even though his job was to prepare her for assistance, he had to recognize how very skilled she was in terms of athletic ability. We still worked with her on her responsibilities as a potential assistance dog, and she worked very well with us. But, her heart never seemed to be in her work, and I, above all, knew how that felt. Kessen always said that not all dogs wanted to be helper dogs, and at this point in Izzy's training, he was absolutely right...or so we thought.

Because I lived vicariously through Izzy's numerous escapades and mischievous endeavors, Izzy often referred to me as her soulmate. She did things that I dreamt of doing yet would never attempt out of fear of being caught. I laughed at her refusals, which was very rude on my part, but Izzy's descriptions of the folks' responses were hilarious. She and I would sit by our kennels at night and just relive her escapades of the day. If athletic glory were what Izzy truly wanted, I hoped her dream would come true. But, sometimes dreams change, and I hoped that Izzy would keep an open mind and recognize new opportunities that arose during her stay with us.

In an attempt to add variety to Izzy's life of training, the folks enrolled her in an agility course. Izzy was in her glory and thought the folks finally understood her true calling. Izzy loved the agility class and excelled on the course in terms of speed and accuracy. The folks now knew she had the ability to be a champion in the agility setting.

But, an interesting thing happened to Izzy on the road to glory. She met a number of assistance dogs along the way at dog walks and fund raisers and somehow realized that helping others just might be a better road to travel as opposed to the one for championship glory. She had a lot to think about in terms of her future and hoped that she'd make the right decision when the time came.

In her final agility competition, Izzy won...paws down...with the highest scores. Everyone, including Kessen who had accepted her career goal weeks ago, was happy for Izzy and thought she'd go on to win more and more awards in the future. She'd have to report to Puppy College first, but if her heart weren't in it, she'd be released from the program and could resume her promising career in agility

However, Izzy's next decision took both of us by surprise. Even though her dream of winning a first-place ribbon and a championship trophy came true, she decided that dreams come in many forms and can change along the way...sometimes for the better. Going to Puppy College was her new dream, and she was determined to be successful in terms of assistance to someone. As a token of our friendship, she left her first-place ribbon for me because I was a good friend to her as well as her soulmate. To further demonstrate her kindness and consideration, the winning blue ribbon was appropriately

Another success story...

placed on the kennel wall in accordance with my belief in *feng shui*. She left her championship trophy for the folks to keep on their mantle as a reminder of her training time in the household, and off she went to Puppy College where a career in assistance awaited her. What a wonderful journey this audacious, puppy-turned-responsible dog had in our household. She entered as a Black Tornado and left for a world of assistance. Now, that was a success story for our Socialization Squad's résumé. Izzy's stay with us was a real test of the Socialization Squad's mentoring, but we proved to be up to the challenge. We had renewed confidence in our ability to work with any and all types of puppies. When would we learn that being overconfident only leads to trouble?

Tansy's Return

As it happened, we didn't have to wait very long for our next encounter with the bizarre. Tansy, the good-time girl and party-pup, was coming back to our house for assistance training. Her original puppy raisers were moving out of state and couldn't take her along, so our folks agreed to take over Tansy's training. Kessen and I just looked at each other and realized that without Izzy here as our designated puppy sitter, Tansy's mentoring was left up to us. Once again, the Socialization Squad was activated and ready to begin the training program.

Tansy was a high-energy puppy and wasn't afraid to let the world know it. She was busy every minute of the day. Mom often had her in a time-out in the kitchen, but that quiet time only served as a means of renewing her energy. By default, I was mostly in charge of her house behavior while Kessen attended to what he considered pack leader responsibilities. I wasn't sure what those duties actually were, but they seemed to require a lot of sleeping on his part. Being in charge really had its perks!

Tansy, being in perpetual motion all day long, was given the nickname of Wiggle Butt which was not only cute but also very appropriate. Tansy didn't fully appreciate it until our mom happened to give her a new nickname: T-T-Pinquay. We thought the T-T came from her given name, but where did Pinquay come from? It didn't make sense, but sometimes our mom said things that didn't jive with the dog world. It was just another of those oddities between canine and human worlds...it might not make sense but was acceptable in both worlds.

Jet propelled...

While I truly lived vicariously through Izzy's escapades, Tansy had a special place in my heart. We were such opposites...high energy versus low-keyed, yet we got along so well together. When Tansy was sequestered in the kitchen for a time out, I would often lay in a down position by the gate right next to her. Tansy, wanting something to do, would often volunteer to lick my ears as a sign of friendship. Being such a delightful diva and fully committed to being pampered, how could I refuse? It certainly wasn't the equivalent of a mani-pawdi but still a very enjoyable experience. So, Tansy would lick away for a while, and then I'd turn my head so she'd get the other ear. After all, ears came in pairs. Kessen, watching from the other room, just rolled his eyes due to my taking advantage of Tansy for ear cleansing. He often asked if I felt guilty about having Tansy assist with my beauty regimen, and my response was always...not one bit. Tansy was learning unique techniques for good grooming, and I was just doing my part to assist in her learning process.

But Tansy wasn't a goodie-four-paws all of the time. She had a sense of humor and was quite the prankster. On one occasion, while I was wearing a soft cone from a surgical procedure, Tansy tricked me during a contest of imitating commands. She would do a command and have me duplicate it. We often did this while Tansy was in training, and it was a fun game.

I was happy to have my mind occupied following my procedure and was grateful for Tansy's suggestion of a game. We were both positioned on throw rugs, and as Tansy sat, I imitated her. When Tansy stood up, I did the same. Then, Tansy went into a down position on her throw rug. I matched her action as quickly as possible. As soon as I flattened myself on the throw rug, I realized that she had tricked me. Because I was wearing Kessen's soft cone from one of his past surgical procedures, it was a bit too large for me and had sections of Velcro exposed on the sides. With my imitation of Tansy's down position, I found myself stuck to the throw rug. Tansy was rolling

Not so funny ...

around the floor with laughter since I was tightly pinned to the rug on the floor. Within a very few minutes, the folks found me and quickly determined that Tansy was to blame for my predicament. While Tansy was sequestered in her kennel for the evening, I saw her laughing through the wires. The punishment was definitely worth the crime as far as she was concerned. Truth be told, I wished I had thought of that prank first. It was awesome!

Tansy's stay with us at the sorority house was full of pranks and fun. Kessen didn't always agree with her tactics, but he did have a sense of humor hiding behind that pack leader façade. I, on the other paw, thoroughly appreciated Tansy's enjoyment of life and fun at all costs. She didn't give a hoot about consequences. If and when caught doing something unacceptable, she showed no remorse. That was part of her charm...she smiled in the face of adversity. How I envied that dog!

The most incredible thing that Tansy did to earn her legendary status in the household was something that many dogs had attempted before her but were never successful in doing. While in training, each dog attended Sunday church service with the folks and had to pass the Holy Water Fountain that had blessed water spiraling down into a container. How tempting was that refreshing water after sitting in a down position on the floor while looking only at feet during the church service? It was totally inviting, but the trick was not to get caught if an attempt were made to gulp some water. Kessen, yes...I said Kessen...attempted the Big Gulp when he was in training but was immediately stopped with the snap of his leash by our mom. I never wanted to go for the Big Gulp because I figured in order to do that, I'd have to get some part of my body wet, and that was never going to happen. When Izzy was in training, she thought about attempting the Big Gulp when passing that Holy Water Fountain, but knew she was constantly watched by our mom and didn't have a chance at being successful.

Tansy, recognizing that a caper such as the Big Gulp

needed thought and extensive planning, set out to make it happen. Each week, she'd see that refreshing water just waiting for her to take that drink and knew that when the time was right, she'd execute her plan. Just before she was to leave for Puppy College, the folks took Tansy for her last

History would be made today!

church service. As far as Tansy was concerned, it was now or never. As they were leaving the church, our mom happened to stop to talk with another parishioner. Tansy recognized the opportunity, made her move and took that swig from the Holy Water Fountain. With her successful gulp of that water, Tansy became a legend. To date, that mischievous endeavor known as the Big Gulp Caper has never been duplicated in the history of the sorority house.

After being blessed by the folks' favorite priest, Tansy went off to Puppy College to a life of helping others. After a few years of service, she came back to us to live her life in the security of the sorority house while helping the other pups who crossed the threshold. She had a lot to offer new puppies, and her being here also increased the numbers in our pack. Although he wished for some males to be included, Kessen was still quite pleased with the increasing size of his pack. While he didn't know it at the time, his wish would soon be granted.

Harley

Harley was our mystery dog because he was being co-raised between our folks and another family. We weren't sure how co-raising worked but knew we wouldn't see him every day for training. Believing our Socialization Squad was prepared for any contingency, we'd see how it all played out once we knew Harley's schedule.

Just the knowledge that the sorority house was getting a male puppy was enough to send Kessen into a major tailspin. He was beside himself with excitement and couldn't help hide his pride in gender equality.

Yea for gender equality!

Tansy and I weren't worried because the female attendance

over the years already outweighed the male presence. With Harley's living here, even on a limited basis, we were evenly distributed in terms of gender.

Between Tansy's gusto and my daily beauty routines, we would keep Harley busy the entire time he was here in the sorority house. We'll have him jumping around and looking at his profile in the glass patio doors in no time. Seeing Harley's masculinity reduced to glamor and enthusiasm would drive Kessen wild!

In a strong effort to curb our enthusiasm over Harley's arrival and unique plans for his future, Kessen gave us a rather stern warning about our serious responsibilities to Harley in terms of his future as an assistance dog. Being reminded of our jobs was exactly what we needed to bring us back to reality. Kessen was doing his job as pack leader and gave a rather similar lecture to Harley when he first

arrived...complete with *stink eye*. What surprised us was that Harley actually seemed to listen to Kessen's lecture and looked at Kessen as if he had just met his hero in life. Was that a male bonding thing? Tansy and I just looked puzzled at what had transpired between the two males.

Harley listened.

Harley had a lot going for him in terms of looks and personality. He was a handsome puppy with a coat as black as coal and eyes that glistened with excitement. He might have been a poster pup for the Labrador Retriever breed because he represented all of the breed's best qualities. He wasn't with us much because of the co-raising gig, but when he was here, he was a real male's male. Wrestling with Kessen became a ritual that they both enjoyed, and Tansy and I actually liked watching them roll around on the floor. At first, I was appalled because Harley didn't mind the dust from the floor covering his impeccably well-brushed coat after the wrestling matches. Eventually, I realized that wrestling was just a male-to-male bonding ritual.

Those two dogs getting all sweaty and dusty didn't make any sense to me, but a lot of things that didn't jive with good grooming and daily attention to appearances often eluded my understanding. I just had to accept wrestling as having some relevant value in Harley's development. Of

Wrestle Mania

course, Tansy thoroughly enjoyed seeing their romping and twisting all around the floor. She totally understood the value of burning off high energy in a positive way because, in her mind, that release of energy only encouraged good behavior. Leave it to Tansy to find a sensible rationalization for high energy gone wild!

We thoroughly enjoyed the time Harley spent at the sorority house. He worked diligently on his commands with the folks and represented the assistance organization with pride when out in public with them. Kessen spent time sharing his experiences and leadership skills with Harley, and I focused on good grooming techniques and attention to appearances. Tansy, on the other paw, used her high-energy skills as a means of burning off Harley's so-called puppy energy while in the yard. Even though Tansy wasn't an actual member of the Socialization Squad, we made her an honorary squad sergeant due to her work with Harley. Kessen often acknowledged our good work which made us try even harder to fully prepare Harley for Puppy College. We all had jobs to do, and I must admit, we took them seriously and did them well.

There would be other puppies in our future, but we were ready for each and every one of them. That pesky over-confident spirit seemed to rear its ugly head after each puppy left us for Puppy College. Would we ever learn not to embrace that notion? Based upon past experiences, it doesn't seem likely...

So many puppies crossed the threshold of the sorority house over the years and sharing little tidbits about each of them reminded me of the kinship I shared with Kessen. Working side by side with him gave me a sense of accomplishment and value as a member of the Socialization Squad. While Kessen helped develop those talents in me, I was forever grateful for the lessons learned. However, being the Glamour Girl of the pack will always be my finest accomplishment and legacy to the canine world! Always such drama...

16

The Longest Day

The day started out just like any other day. While looking through the sunroom window, I saw the sun shining brightly, white puffy clouds billowing in the sky, and the grass looking quite a bit greener after being mowed yesterday. The yard, filled with multicolored flowers, looked unusually inviting, and I couldn't wait to go for a romp later in the day.

I loved the tranquility of the yard in the early morning...especially when it looked like it did today. As a puppy, I would often spend hours in the yard either running around or hiding from the folks when they came looking for me. They knew I was playing a game and often made the search seem like a professional Broadway production of Hide and Seek.

Can you see me now?

My favorite hiding place was behind a concrete statue of three puppies that I named Mount Pupsmore. I would scrunch my head on the top of the statue in hopes of not being seen by the folks. Since they made a great deal over not being able to find me when they were right in front of me, I'm sure they knew I was there. I enjoyed that game so much, and I'm sure they did as well. Remembering that particular game gave me such a warm, fuzzy feeling. While I could probably duplicate that hiding position again on that statue, my head was now much too large to go unnoticed.

Because the folks were still sleeping, the house was relatively quiet. Kessen was asleep on the couch, which was his privilege since he was leader of the pack and no longer

in training. Come to think of it... he sure was sleeping a lot lately. Leading a pack of silly dogs like us had to be exhausting. Tansy was bouncing around the house looking for something to do or undo, and I was ready to enjoy a peaceful nap since Harley was at his other house for the weekend. Between the super weather and the serenity in the house, this day

He gets to sleep on the couch.

had the potential of being absolutely perfect.

As I settled in my cushioned bed in preparation for my nap, I thought about the numerous changes that had occurred during the last few months. Kessen had increased my responsibilities with regard to Harley's training. That surprised me because Kessen usually wanted to oversee everything that transpired with the pups in training. Nevertheless, I wasn't going to complain because I enjoyed being in charge. Harley's training was progressing nicely under my direction, and I was getting some invaluable experience in terms of leadership responsibilities. Although Kessen's turning the challenge of Harley's training over to me was surprising, I discovered skills I never knew I had.

Kessen's next move actually shocked me when he chose Tansy as his back-up storyteller to continue his storytelling tradition in the years to come. Kessen was the grand, master storyteller in the neighborhood and was capable of holding a deck full of eager dogs in total suspense while telling his stories. Sharing all of those stories with Tansy was an awesome honor,

Did you hear what Kessen just said?

a huge commitment of time as well as an enormous responsibility. When I heard about Kessen's intentions regarding Tansy, one might have knocked me over with a rubber dog bone. Tansy was just as surprised as I was when she was approached by Kessen.

It was, indeed, a great honor for Tansy to be asked to follow in such a master storyteller's paw prints. While Tansy was truly flattered by Kessen's request, she wondered if my not being asked might upset me. After all, I was second in command of the pack with Tansy in third place. I assured Tansy that a responsibility as great as the storytelling endeavor was never even a consideration for me. That obligation would entail listening to all of Kessen's stories and learning how to hold the attention of a crowd of demanding dogs. Remembering the stories in their proper sequence was also essential.

Yes, that storytelling gig was a huge honor, but it was also a lot of work...hard and intense work. Did any of that sound like it would be something I'd enjoy doing? Kessen knew I wasn't suited for it which is why he chose Tansy for the position. She had a strong work ethic and would work tirelessly to excel as Kessen's back-up storyteller and to follow in Kessen's paw prints when needed. I, on the other paw, had some semblance of a work ethic, but nothing as serious as required for the storytelling position. Kessen, in his wisdom, had chosen wisely and assigned each of us tasks in accordance with our competence. I was as happy as a dog finding a cookie under the couch with my assignment.

Kessen needs a vacation from us!

Tansy and I both knew that Kessen was slowing down a bit, but he had, after all, been responsible for quite a lot during his years as pack leader. We weren't easy pack members to keep in line either. He often reminded us that our constant bickering gave him indigestion, so I guess he unquestionably deserved some relaxation as well as some relief for his digestive tract. Besides, we were excited and quite happy with our newly acquired responsibilities.

With those thoughts in mind, I was just about to fall asleep when the folks woke up and were rushing around the house. It was unusual for such frantic activity so early in the morning. Before we really knew what was happening, they left the house with Kessen. It was very strange because they usually have us go into our kennels in the sunroom, lock the kennel doors and turn on the television for us

What was happening?

before they leave the house. That television left on was meant to fool us into thinking they were still home, but we never believed it. Still, we liked the continuous noise of the television, and sometimes there was a certain program that was enjoyable to watch. In any event, nothing in their ritual was followed today in their rush to leave the house.

As Tansy and I looked at each other, we weren't sure whether to be frightened by the folks' quick departure with Kessen or to take advantage of the newfound freedom in their absence. There were so many temptations available to us that we weren't sure just what to do. Rather than give in to the temptation of a tug-of-war with one of our beds or a dirt fight with dirt from the planter in the corner, we each chose to do something responsible…or at least one of us did.

Not wanting to admit that she was fearful for Kessen's health because of the hasty departure of the folks, Tansy decided to go into her kennel and reminisce about the pictures hanging on the Wall of Fame. That special wall held pictures of all of the dogs who crossed the threshold of the sorority house. I could tell she was worried, but her telling of the stories as Kessen had taught her seemed to help lessen her fears.

I chose a very different method of dealing with my fears regarding Kessen. Much to Tansy's dismay, I chose to defy the rule of no jumping on the furniture and found a comfortable spot on the couch where Kessen had slept.

Tansy shared stories from the Wall of Fame.

Being near his scent brought me a bit closer to him. Somehow, Tansy felt accountable for my lapse in couch behavior, but she had nothing to worry about. I'd take full responsibility for my actions when the folks brought Kessen home. I really had no choice regarding ownership in the matter since my blonde fur would be all over the couch. That was hard evidence of the crime and very difficult to deny.

While wanting to limit my fears by sleeping, I just couldn't get comfortable on the couch. Knowing something might be wrong with Kessen was much too disturbing for restful positioning on the couch cushions. As I listened to Tansy's melodic voice from the sunroom talking about Turin, who was the first dog to cross the threshold of the sorority house, I found myself drifting into sleep surrounded by Kessen's scent on the couch. Perhaps Tansy was going to talk about all of the dogs whose pictures were on the wall. If she did that, I'd probably be asleep for a long, long time. That dog could talk!

When Tansy saw what I was doing, I knew she

I felt closer to Kessen up here on the couch.

thought I was being defiant by disregarding the furniture rule, but I really wasn't. It was just my way of dealing with my fears about Kessen. I knew Tansy was upset about the folks leaving so quickly with Kessen because she kept looking at the clock on the wall. Doing that was an exercise in futility since she couldn't tell time. Instead, I think she relied on the position of the sun and the amount of daylight streaming through the windows as a means of telling the time of day.

After a while, I woke up from my restless nap and, once again, threw caution to the wind and jumped on the love seat. That was totally brave because that item of furniture would be the first thing our parents saw as they took us out to the dog run. I still didn't care about the consequences of my actions. I just wanted Kessen to come home and be well. His scent was so very comforting that I risked all sorts of consequences.

It was getting very late in the day, and the folks still weren't home with Kessen. This situation had to be very serious for them to be gone so long with us unattended. Thank goodness Harley was at his other home for the weekend. In his youthful state, he'd be wreaking havoc all over the house when not kenneled. That pup wasn't prepared for self-restraint!

As it got dark outside, I realized that it was way beyond our regular feeding time. I meandered over to the food bowls and decided to stand over the food bowls as a means of making food somehow appear out of nowhere. In my mind, keeping with the regular routine of the day would make things all right. I know it didn't make any sense, but it was all I could think of to make Kessen come home to us. Tansy thought I was insensitive because I was thinking of food when something must be wrong with Kessen, but she was very wrong about her conclusion. I was just trying to keep the routine so he'd come back to us and be well.

Since the folks didn't have time to leave a light on when they left so suddenly with Kessen, it was not only dark outside but also inside the house as well. The only light came from the neighbor's porch light, and that only gave a bit of brightness in the sunroom. The rest of the house was very dark and cast an ominous tone to the day's events.

Since standing over the food bowls didn't bring the folks home, I went out to the utility room and just sat facing the door. I was convinced that staring at that door would certainly make their coming home happen. I don't know how long I sat there, but suddenly, I heard the garage door opening. While I stood up from my sitting position, Tansy came running into the utility room to greet the folks and Kessen. As the door opened, our mom warned us not to jump on Kessen because he had a surgical procedure, needed his rest and would be fine in a few days. We were so relieved until we saw this huge cone on his head preventing him from licking the bandage around his stomach. What had happened to our fearless leader of the pack?

As Kessen walked slowly to his bed, he looked at us and realized that we had been on our own during the day and didn't destroy anything. He mentioned how proud he was of us and always knew we could function in an orderly manner if left unsupervised. Fortunately, he didn't pass the couch and loveseat that were almost totally covered with bits of my blonde coat. I gave Tansy a wry smile just to let her know that I had gotten away with my sleeping on the furniture. She just shook her head in disbelief...she always got caught when she did something wrong while I remained unscathed!

We were just so happy that Kessen was going to be okay and that we had pretty much lived up to his

This was quite a stressful day!

expectations in terms of behavior when unattended. We learned a lot about each other from today's experience in terms of handling stress and concern for one another. While we had our differences, we both agreed that it was by far the longest day we ever shared...

On this particular day, Tansy and I were both extremely worried about Kessen, but each of us handled the stress in our own unique ways. By telling Kessen's stories from the pictures on the Wall of Fame, Tansy was able to deal with her apprehension and concern for him as well as delve into her first experience in storytelling. Sharing those stories brought her closer to him.

I, on the other paw, chose to disregard rules and be closer to Kessen in my own way by sleeping on the furniture in his favorite spots. Tansy didn't understand my way of coping because it involved disregarding rules, but I fully understood hers. We were different in so many ways, but our concern for Kessen's well-being was the same, and that's exactly how it should be.

17

Season of Surprises

In a few days, Kessen seemed much healthier and was moving around the house quite easily. We were able to be around him, but he still couldn't do any running in the yard. He wanted to talk with us about a serious matter and scheduled one of his lecture sessions. As we waited silently for some new rule in the sorority house or a change in routine for the sake of

Serious Business

efficiency, we were absolutely flabbergasted when Kessen

Dawson

approached the topic of his retirement. In the near future, he planned to go to an exclusive place called the Rainbow Bridge. Kessen said it was a place for all leaders of the pack to meet for an eternity of tranquility, camaraderie and all the treats they could eat. He might even be reunited with his two good friends, Dawson and Echo, who visited the sorority house on various occasions

when they were both puppies. What a fantastic get-together that would be. I imagined what great fun they would have… especially the part about the endless treats.

The Rainbow Bridge sounded like such a great place, and Tansy and I wondered if we might visit him there.

Echo might be there.

Kessen thought our visiting wasn't such a good idea. Tansy thought Kessen didn't want us to visit because the retirement place was only for pack leaders, and they just didn't want any subordinates messing up the place and eating their treats. I thought she might be totally correct in that assumption, but I still didn't want Kessen to leave us. He assured me that, in his absence, I was ready for any sort of responsibility that came my way. An additional surprise came when Kessen told me that when he left, I was to assume the position of leader of the pack.

What did he just say?

New leader of the pack? Me? That new information dropped me to the kennel floor as well as caused Tansy to look for escape options for this most unusual decision on Kessen's part. Within minutes, Tansy narrowed her flight options to hiding somewhere in the house or running away from home. She also gave consideration to the possibility that Kessen's decision was part of a nightmare, and she just had to wake up for this new leader of the pack nonsense to go away. Apparently, she had no faith in Kessen's choice nor in my ability to lead this pack. Part of me had to concur with Tansy's logic but would never admit it to her.

Kessen reassured me that for the last few months he had been giving me additional responsibilities with Harley, and I handled them with ease. He knew I was ready...if and when he left for retirement. I was still skeptical while Tansy was wondering if she had to bow in my presence or call me Her Royal Highness if Kessen ever left, and I assumed the leadership position. Those options were intolerable to Tansy, but I was grateful that she brought them to my attention. Having me actually thinking about those options frightened Tansy even more.

Tansy was given the honor of being Kessen's back-up storyteller if and when he retired. For months, he had been preparing her, and she was doing quite well. She listened attentively during story after story and had great recall of the sequence of events as told by Kessen. Nevertheless, what happened next floored both of us...Kessen gave his smelly, precious ring toy to Tansy for safe keeping. She was actually driven to tears when that occurred. I thought the tears were partially due to the smelly aspect of the toy, but I'm sure they were mostly due to the sentiment of the gift. Tansy was so appreciative of that gift that she kept it in her kennel for safe keeping. I had my own views about the toy's kennel placement but kept them to myself. It was, indeed, a great gift from Kessen, and truth be told, I was a bit envious of his not offering it to me.

While Kessen's designated changes took us totally off guard, he made those choices based upon our proven skills. In spite of what we might have thought at the time, he always seemed to know what was best for us, and that ability made him such a great pack leader. Although we

219

often dreaded his stern lectures and weekly seminars about appropriate behavior, rules and regulations, Kessen always ended those sessions with thoughts and reflections about life. One of his most notable thoughts dealt with living a good life, working hard but making sure to take the time to smell the flowers. I wasn't quite sure what he meant at first, but sometime later, his wise words of wisdom tumbled around my mind with such clarity and guided my life.

Always take time to smell the flowers.

We didn't think very much of Kessen's decisions regarding our own futures until a few weeks later when the folks suddenly had to leave the house with Kessen. Just as they were about to leave, Kessen stopped, gave us a brief nod and a warm smile to let us know that he'd be okay. Hours later, the folks returned without him. We knew something was very wrong because both of them had been crying. Then, we realized that Kessen had gone to his retirement home at the Rainbow Bridge. We hoped that he was now enjoying the company of the other pack leaders and the endless treats. He definitely earned that all-inclusive environment.

Even knowing he had those perks didn't minimize the sadness we felt over his leaving. After thinking about everything that Kessen had discussed with us over the past few weeks, we realized that he had been saying goodbye to us all along. We just didn't want to accept it.

Weeks passed, and the folks were getting ready for the holiday season. This would be our first holiday without our dear Kessen, and the entire family missed him terribly. When our mom hung our red, glittered Christmas stockings on the mantle and placed a beautiful gold bow on the space where Kessen's stocking would have been, I felt such overpowering sadness. Tansy felt the same sadness since she had tears in her eyes every time she passed the mantle. When sunlight filtering through the window touched that gold bow in a certain way, the bow seemed to sparkle.

There wasn't too much joy in the household this year. Pretty soon Harley would be going to Puppy College, and our pack would dwindle to just the two of us. Tansy refused to call me Her Royal Highness nor would she bow in my presence. She did, however, respect Kessen's wishes and did whatever I requested of her with regard to the pack order...within reason.

We didn't feel much like rekindling Marnie's Tradition of Turmoil for the Christmas photo. It just didn't seem right, and surprisingly, the folks seemed to feel the same way. Because of the lack of Christmas spirit in the household, no photo was taken at all.

There was just no laughter in the house anymore. In an effort to change the atmosphere in the house, Dad tried to add some Christmas cheer by purchasing a freshly-cut tree. It was a Frasier Fir and had dark blue-green needles with branches that turned a bit upward giving it a fuller effect. It certainly wasn't as large as the artificial tree of last year, but it was beautifully shaped and also extremely fragrant.

Tansy, Harley and I sat around while our dad attempted to get that tree standing perfectly upright in the tree-stand. He kept rotating that tree around while our mom gave her opinion as she moved from one side of the room to the other. Finally, the tree was perfectly positioned. With perfection accomplished in terms of an upright tree, our dad collapsed on the floor as if he were totally exhausted from the activity. Seeing him fooling around like that was our signal to enter into the fun. All three of us jumped on top of our dad while Mom looked on and laughed. It was the first laughter heard in the house since Kessen left us. Hearing that laughter for the first time in such a long time made us pause from our assault on Dad to enjoy the moment, but then we quickly resumed the activity. Now, everyone was laughing, and for the first time, it felt like the Christmas spirit was returning to the house. Our folks began decorating the tree with twinkling lights, shiny gold bows and vibrant red ornaments of various sizes. We looked on in amazement as the tree was systematically transformed into a dazzling image of beauty and splendor.

During the night before Christmas, Tansy and I heard our mom rummaging around in the living room. We thought the tree had been totally decorated so she must have been doing something else. Because we were so exhausted from all of the fun during the day, both of us just figured we'd see what she had done in the morning. Neither of us bothered to look to see what she was up to in the middle of the night.

Morning came, and after our ritual of going out to the dog run before eating, we were momentarily startled by the appearance of the tree. Tansy stopped so suddenly that I bumped into her causing Harley to bump into me. What was so different, and why did the tree look so extra special?

It was perfect!

As it turned out, our mom had added some very special ornaments to the tree. The tree branches held silver paw-print picture frames with our very own unique pictures in them. What a wonderful surprise! While thoughts of Kessen not being able to see this wonderful Christmas tree filled my mind, Tansy voiced her opinion for all to hear regarding his absence by howling. Harley kept nudging us to listen to what he had to tell us, but sad to say, we rarely listened to him…even on a good day.

Because he wouldn't relent with his pushing and shoving, we finally asked Harley what was so important for him to act in this manner? With a triumphant smile on his face, he told us to look at the very top of the tree…just under the angel. Reluctantly, Tansy and I did what we were told and there, at the very top, was the silver paw-print picture frame with our dear Kessen's photo. Thanks to Harley's perseverance, we now knew that Kessen was with us on this special tree and would be with us for the rest of our lives during the Christmas season.

That day, guests came to share holiday cheer as well as reminisce about Kessen and all of the wonderful things he did for others. Harley, Tansy and I listened attentively as we gnawed on tasty dog bones and treats given to us by the guests. One of the guests, in particular, mentioned that she believed that an animal's spirit could move on in the next world to accomplish an unfulfilled goal or even reach a dream that

Kessen was here with us.

never came true. She was certain that happened with humans as well. Tansy and I were both skeptical of that notion, and Harley was just too busy gnawing on his bone to give it any serious thought. Nevertheless, having guests in the house again was fun, and the holiday season ended much too soon for us.

Everyone loved Kessen.

There were so many changes forthcoming in our futures. Kessen's choosing me for the top position of leader of the pack sent Tansy into hiding over the possibility of her becoming an indentured servant. His teaching Tansy the masterful technique of storytelling was such an honor. That skill gave Tansy the opportunity to fulfill her destiny of carrying on his tradition by following in his awesome paw prints.

Losing Kessen was, of course, the biggest surprise of all, and one that threw the household into the depths of sadness. What would the members of the sorority house do without Kessen? He was the skilled leader, the gentle arbitrator and loyal friend who held us all together not only as a pack but also as a family. While missing him left such a void in all of us, keeping his memory close to our hearts and remembering all he had done for us would help our family move forward. In a short period of time, we encountered so many unexpected changes in our lives which only proved that this holiday season was, indeed, a most unusual season of surprises...

In spite of not having Kessen with us this holiday season, we somehow struggled through it and managed to regain the joy of the season with our family. Doing that together was one of the biggest surprises... especially after losing Kessen. Realizing that he would always be in our hearts, remembering his stories as well as having him looking down at us from that silver paw-print picture frame every Christmas made this the most memorable season of all.

18

New Beginnings

The holidays were over, and it was time for Harley to leave for Puppy College. He had matured into such a wonderful dog. What was interesting about Harley was that he seemed to share certain characteristics from each of the dogs who lived in the sorority house. He demonstrated leadership skills similar to Kessen's, excelled in athletic ability following Izzy's example and enjoyed helping others

Harley represented each of us.

just like Marnie. His charming personality and good grooming techniques were unquestionably attributed to my fashionista-like mentorship, and his masterful use of silly pranks was certainly a reflection of Tansy's influence. Tansy even joked that in a strange sense, Harley was taking all of us to Puppy College with him. Kessen, having such an awful experience in Puppy College, would not have been pleased to hear that!

As we prepared for the trip to the training facility with Harley, the folks were asked by the trainers of the organization if they'd have room in their car to bring a graduating dog back to his partner. They were happy to accommodate and knew we'd definitely have room in the car.

We said our goodbyes to Harley in the car because he knew the tradition of not looking back once handed over to the trainer. While a part of us felt sad to see him go, he was more than ready for the experience. He was headed for greatness in terms of assistance, and we were just happy to have been a part of his journey.

As we prepared to leave, our mom went to get the dog who was going to be our traveling companion on the trip home. Tansy and I were eager to meet him, and I made it a point to shake my coat to achieve that feathered look that added to my already dazzling appearance. Tansy just rolled her eyes at what she considered my shameless attempt to attract any and all males looking for a Good-Time Girl. Tansy was just jealous because she had to rely on her personality to attract males. I, on the other paw, just had to be me!

What a handsome dog!

As Mom approached the car, both Tansy and I did a double take. Our traveling companion was a cream-colored dog with retriever-like characteristics. I had only seen a dog slightly resembling that breed when the family visited North Carolina many years ago.

Demonstrating a great level of confidence, our traveling companion jumped into the back seat of the car and assumed the middle position which was traditionally reserved for the leader of the pack. Since he was a guest and a gorgeous one at that, I overlooked what might have been construed as a lack of recognition of my leadership position. Tansy was having a good laugh about our guest taking the middle position, but I mentioned that he was entitled to certain privileges because of the situation. I think Tansy just knew I was in my flirting mode, and protocol went out the door when that happened.

There was something very extraordinary about this traveler, and it had nothing to do with his gorgeous appearance. His name was Charlie, and he was an English Cream Golden Retriever. We did, however, laugh when he said his name because our dad's name was Charles, and his friends called him Charlie. Since we were already laughing as we left the driveway, we knew this trip going home would be fun.

Tansy also sensed something.

Tansy and I were totally fascinated by this traveler. He was impeccably groomed which added to his stately appearance, but there was just something special about him. Was it the way he looked at each of us or the twinkle in his eyes that suggested a form of closeness to us? I just couldn't put my paw on it.

Tansy also seemed to feel something as well as she sat next to Charlie, but she didn't share her feelings with me. She just kept looking at Charlie

229

in a curious way as if she were trying to figure out where she had met him in the past.

While driving, Charlie put his head on our dad's shoulder just as Kessen did when enjoying a car-ride. While I thought it might be significant, most dogs probably did the same thing while riding in a car. Charlie also turned his head to give our mom a bit of a light kiss on her cheek while they traveled the highway. Even our mom was looking at Charlie and trying to figure out if she had met this wonderful dog in the past.

As we got closer to Charlie's destination, I couldn't let go of the feeling that Charlie and I had met before. But, it just didn't make any sense because I only met a female dog of his breed years ago when the folks took Kessen and me to North Carolina. I surely would have remembered meeting a dog as gorgeous and impressive as Charlie.

We reached our destination, and Charlie was getting ready to leave the car. He looked at each of us in such a strange way...as if we shared some sort of kinship. His insightful glance our way seemed to indicate that he acknowledged us as familiar, and at the same time, was saying goodbye once again...for good.

I didn't know what to think as Charlie left the car, but when he passed me by, the closeness I felt to him was so intense...yet totally unexplainable. I wanted to share my thoughts with Tansy, but she would just think I was carrying on about another opportunity for lost love. So, I said nothing to anybody, but the nagging feeling of knowing that dog named Charlie wasn't going away.

As Charlie walked up the driveway to his new life of

Kessen's spirit lives on in Charlie.

assistance to a young boy, he suddenly stopped and looked back at us. As he tilted his head a certain way, looked directly into our eyes and grinned a bit, I immediately knew with absolute certainty that this stately, magnificent dog staring back at us was Kessen's spirit in Charlie's body. But, wasn't that concept impossible? Was that guest at Christmas time accurate when she believed that a dog's spirit could move on in another life to reach an unfulfilled goal? Kessen's goal was always to help one special person in need as an assistance dog, but he never got to fulfill that goal because of his release from Puppy College. After having given us that telling glance and grin, Charlie turned and walked the remaining way to his new life of assistance to a young boy.

I could never tell Tansy that I believed it was Kessen's spirit in the body of the gorgeous English Cream Golden Retriever. She'd revoke her membership in our pack once and for all. Tansy frequently threatened to do that since I was given that leadership position, but now she'd have grounds to prove that I was no longer of sound mind. I decided to keep my thoughts of Kessen to myself but was so happy that Kessen had the opportunity to finally fulfill his goal of helping one special person in need. Perhaps, I would share my thoughts with Tansy at a later date…when and if the right moment ever came along. I really couldn't be sure of anything after that experience.

We will honor Kessen by living kind and loving lives.

It seemed as if we were all facing new beginnings with regard to the changes and responsibilities in our lives. If one believed as I did, even Kessen's spirit was given another chance to fulfill his dream. We weren't puppies any more, and Kessen prepared us well for the future. Tansy and I would use these new beginnings to make him proud wherever he was. That was my sincere promise to him...

Having me take over the role of leader of the pack was the most surprising decision Kessen ever made, and passing his skill of storytelling on to Tansy was his best decision. Both Kessen and Tansy told their versions of the events in a most memorable manner. Kessen would have been proud of Tansy because she definitely mastered the art of storytelling. Through her storytelling expertise, Tansy confirmed that she actually listened to Kessen during his lectures. While my version of this story varied a bit from theirs, in theory, the events were essentially the same.

CONCLUSION

Ten years ago, I was just a puppy in training at the sorority house and never thought I'd ever be in this leadership position. I certainly didn't have the best track record in terms of a work ethic. In fact, I probably took shirking responsibility to an art form. However, over the years, Kessen apparently saw something in my development that pointed to my being the right choice for taking over his position as leader of the pack. Believe me, it was more of a shock to me than it was to any other member of the family.

I had so much to do.

As the new leader of the pack, I had to be runway-ready at all times, and that task took continuous preparation. Kessen always reminded us to be prepared for the unexpected because stuff happened. In light of his trusted words of wisdom, maintaining my ever-popular, stylish appearance at all cost was just following in his magnificent paw prints. However, I couldn't allow my beauty regimen to interfere with my duties as the new pack leader. Just saying that title of *pack leader* gave me an almost euphoric feeling as it rolled off my delicately-formed pink tongue. To me, the new status was as close to being a queen as I'd ever get. Maybe dreams do come true...

At first, I didn't want to make too many changes or demands of Tansy since she openly compared my leadership role as being similar to a nightmare following eating too much grass in the yard. First, I had to win her over to my way of thinking. However, that task wasn't easy since fluttering eyelashes and demure looks didn't faze her one bit. As it was, she thought my using beauty and feminine wiles to get my way was frivolous, so using my girlish charms wasn't going to go very far with her. Instead, I'd be forced to use either my effective powers of persuasion or bribery...which ever worked the best. I decided to appeal to her intellectual side and convince her that she was an invaluable member of the pack and as such needed the

Tansy was promoted.

proper recognition and change in status.

For that to work, I needed to make my very first executive decision as pack leader and make it a memorable one. Accordingly, I officially promoted Tansy to the top position of co-captain of the Socialization Squad. She previously held an honorary position, but now her status was official and certified by me...the new pack leader. This job promotion was significant because a new puppy was coming to the sorority house, and we'd work together as a team to prepare this new puppy for a life of assistance.

While Tansy appreciated the new position, she knew there were strings attached to this new directive. Tansy probably thought that she'd have to do all of the work herself with the puppy because I was the leader of the pack and as such, had to devote all of my time to maintaining my stately appearance. Sometimes, Tansy just knew exactly what was going to happen before it happened, and her powers of perception were usually quite accurate. I reassured her that we would divide the responsibilities with this new puppy based upon our individual strengths. I'm not sure Tansy believed that at the time, but for credibility's sake, I did not flutter my eyelashes...although it was tempting to do so.

My expertise was, of course, in the areas of maintaining a fashionable appearance, sharing beauty techniques and developing manners in the home. Tansy excelled at teaching and maintaining household and public rules and regulations. She controlled a puppy's running, pushing, shoving and shredding of toys better than any dog I knew. The Puppy Training Seminars, which were originally Kessen's duties, were also assigned to her since she was not only well versed in the procedures but was also capable of effectively giving the *stink eye*. I gave that eye-catching task to her because the squinting required for that technique would undoubtedly cause wrinkles on my face, and I certainly couldn't afford to have that happen. In addition to the important responsibilities as the leader of the pack, I also had to maintain my image as a runway-ready beauty queen at all times!

Tansy accepted the responsibilities as the true team player that she was. However, she refused to refer to me as Her Royal Highness, rejected bowing when in my presence and walked away when I asked her to look into having the initials HRH put on my food bowl and kennel mats. I might have considered that refusal as insubordination on her part,

Welcome Nixie!

but I needed her to fulfill the other tasks as specified earlier. She'd eventually come around to my way of thinking...at least I hoped she would.

The special day of the new puppy's arrival finally came. The newcomer was a petite, black Labrador Retriever from the N Litter. Dad chose the name of Nixie, and our mom thought it was the perfect name for that tiny pup. Her coat, while black as coal, was soft and fluffy, but what one noticed first was the size of her paws. They were perfectly shaped but a bit large. I'm sure she needed them for balance and would eventually grow into them, but for now, they were quite impressive. Physically, she was the perfect little bundle of puppy-fun waiting to happen.

In addition to those special features, what struck me the most was the innocent expression on her tiny face, and for some reason, my thoughts drifted to thinking about Kessen and his missing this wonderful moment. He knew what it felt like to meet a newcomer for the first time, to recognize that hopeful look in a puppy's eyes as well as grasping the tremendous obligation of its care. Seeing this puppy for the first time, I experienced all of those identical feelings. Realizing the tremendous obligation regarding this small tyke's training for the next twelve months triggered a momentary lapse into a full panic mode. I was supposed to be in

Nixie trusted us.

charge, but somehow, I did not have a clue as to what to do.

This little pup didn't care about appearances or beauty techniques. She was in a new home and missing

Benelli

Benelli, her loving birth mother, as well as her wonderful sister named Naomi. This new puppy also unexpectedly faced living with two very different dogs. How frightening that had to be for her in this strange environment. Her fragile expression touched my heart, and I seemed to rise to the occasion. Maybe the reaction to her innocence was what Kessen meant when he assured me that when the time came, I would know what to do.

Naomi

I welcomed this little puppy to the sorority house, reassured her that she would be loved in this wonderful house and then, introduced her to Tansy. I would have introduced her to

241

Tansy sooner, but I didn't want to frighten her any more than she already was. We immediately greeted each other with appropriate sniffing, and judging from Nixie's relaxed state, it was apparent that she was feeling a bit better. The Socialization Squad was officially activated, and Nixie's training began.

Nixie seemed like one of the most enthusiastic pups who came to the sorority house for training. Tansy and I quickly dubbed her The Noodle because of her ability to slide into unique spots that were not easily accessible. That flexibility enabled her to evade our reach on a number of occasions. She often slept under her bed, but perhaps it was just cooler in that strange position.

This pup was flexible!

Nixie was a fast learner but didn't care too much about her appearance. She often dozed off during my training sessions regarding facial care and tooth brushing. Tansy excused Nixie from any consequence because she believed that even the plants dozed off during my lessons. Tansy liked to joke around a lot, and I knew she was just kidding with that remark, but accusing me of being the reason for the plants sleeping was really hitting below the collar. What ever happened to the rule regarding total respect of the pack leader? She wouldn't have done that to Kessen...not even on a good day. But then again, I wasn't Kessen, and Tansy knew I wouldn't give the *stink eye* because of the possibility of wrinkling my flawless face.

Nixie was so special.

As the weeks and months passed, Tansy and I watched Nixie grow and mature into quite the polite, young dog. She was most impressive in terms of learning her commands, wore her cape in the most fashionable manner and was an excellent ambassador for the organization in all public places. What thoroughly pleased Tansy was the fact that Nixie never once even thought about attempting to sneak a drink the from the Holy Water Fountain in church. Tansy's renowned Big Gulp Caper's legacy remained intact.

Because she was housebroken at the tender age of three months, Nixie exceeded expectations and was legendary for not ever having an accident in the house. On the other paw, out of all of the dogs who stayed at the sorority house, she held the record for totally destroying the most dog beds in a twelve-month period. She actually demonstrated a distorted sense of pride regarding that achievement which I believe came from Tansy's teachings. When Tansy was a pup in training, she showed no remorse for any infraction of the rules. Often smiling at being caught in some form of mischief, Tansy must have shared that sense of accomplishment with Nixie.

Nixie was leaving us in a few weeks for Puppy College, and our first endeavor as a team in the Socialization Squad was ending. All in all, Tansy and I worked very well together and, in many respects, looked forward to our next attempt at preparing a puppy for potential assistance. Sure, we had our disagreements in terms of teaching techniques, but our differences were what made us successful. While Tansy's totally ridiculous, plant-dozing insinuation caused a momentary bit of uncertainty, I refused to believe that I put the plants to sleep with my lessons!

Working with Tansy also made me realize how very much I had learned about myself over the years. So much happened since my puppy days in sunny California. I was a distrustful, somewhat mean and loud puppy and, with Kessen's help and guidance, eventually became his choice for leader of the pack. Ten years in this wonderful house filled with the love of my folks, Kessen, Izzy, Marnie, Tansy and Nixie made a huge difference not just in my

Bart - My Handsome Hero

life, but in the lives of all of the dogs who crossed the threshold with their hopes and dreams. I even saw my brother Bart at a fund raiser a few weeks ago, and our reunion was so very special. He recognized me right away, and we spent so much time trading our life's experiences. I might also add that he was still very handsome!

Tansy still carries on Kessen's legacy with her versions of his stories as part of her night time event. She is especially happy when the sky seems devoid of stars, the wind is blowing through the trees and the moon's shadow casts an ominous glow on the deck. Such a dramatic setting for storytelling, and yet, I thought I was the one with the flair for drama! However, Tansy does tell a great story, and the visiting dogs just love her enthusiastic presentations.

This past month, my fashionable, therapy-dog cape was taken out of storage for a reunion with my first love named Rufus. We volunteered at an assisted living facility and had quite a good time with the residents. It was just like old times...he did his tricks while I looked gorgeous. He's just as handsome as he was years ago and is still very much a Babe Magnet!

I've experienced so many wonderful events in my

He's still such a Babe Magnet!

life, and sharing stories in this very first brunch event has been such fun for me. In the months to come, I will be anxious to continue my storytelling in the brunch setting with the dogs in the neighborhood. That mid-morning brunch format just barks of elegance to me.

This evening, my mom told me that she is writing a book about my life and using my stories from the brunch event as the basis for her book. She's written other books about Kessen, Izzy and Tansy and, much to my displeasure, I've only had a supporting role in each of her books. I have

I finally have a starring role!

been a best friend to the leader of the pack, a soulmate to an athletic dreamer and the star of a chapter devoted to me in Tansy's stories about the pictures on the Wall of Fame. I've always been the bridesmaid but never the bride...until now. I'm finally her main character...the spotlight is on me as I take center stage for all to see. I'm really anxious to read her version of my life and hope it does me justice by adequately describing my diva-like personality, extraordinary fashion sense and unique flair for the dramatic.

Sharing my stories with you today in the brunch setting has been such fun for me. I wish Kessen were here to critique my presentations. I owe so much to him for his guidance, patience and tolerance of me as his second in command of the pack. As I look through the sunroom windows and see Tansy and Nixie jaw sparring and air snapping with each other in the yard, I realize how much I

Kessen prepared me for this awesome position!

have changed over the past ten years. There was a time when I'd be right out there with them participating in the fun. But, here I am overseeing the friendly chaos as part of my job as a responsible leader of the pack...just as Kessen was. Even though I didn't realize it during those years, he was preparing me for making the right choices.

While Kessen's excellence in leadership will never be duplicated, I now believe that I am, for the most part, on the right track for following in his paw prints. Because of Kessen's example, I will be kind to others, impeccably groomed, fashionably dressed, runway-ready and will always take the time to smell the flowers. Kessen's legacy is mine to pass on to another dog in the years to come. In my heart, I truly believe Kessen would approve...

I hope you, the reader, have enjoyed my sharing of stories in **Brunch With Brightie**. *So much of my life was influenced by Kessen's teachings, but his most important lessons involved living life to its fullest. I think I am doing just what he wished and doing it quite well! Don't you?*

I'm taking Kessen's advice…enjoying life and having a ball!

The Storyteller

My given name is Brighton, but most people just call me Brightie. I've had quite an interesting life that dates back ten years. That's right...ten years! I'm really quite shy, do not like getting my paws wet but do enjoy spending time with my family and friends. Unfortunately, shiny floors still frighten me.

I came from California, and because of my unfriendly puppy behaviors, I was the only puppy who had the potential of being sent back to the organization. However, I turned my life around with the help of my very best friend named Kessen and my folks. I enjoyed working in the assisted therapy programs with Kessen, but my working with the diverse puppies as co-captain of the Socialization Squad still remains my most heartwarming experience.

This summer, the folks are taking me on a road trip to the Badlands. At first, I thought they were taking me to the dog park, but I was mistaken. It's an actual road trip to South Dakota, and I'm so looking forward to it. Perhaps, I'll even write about it in a blog. After all, anything is possible...

The Author

    Jennifer Rae Trojan, who writes as Jennifer Rae, lives in a suburb of Chicago, Illinois with her husband Chuck and her dog named Brightie. Since retirement as high school guidance counselors, Jennifer and Chuck work with various assistance organizations serving as puppy raisers, puppy sitters and volunteers with animal assisted therapy. In addition to these activities, Jennifer gives presentations at libraries, in schools and to community groups regarding the journey of the assistance dog and how it relates to the writing of her books. Chuck and Brightie, representing two of the characters in all of her books, accompany her to the presentations. Jennifer and her husband consider being a part of a potential assistance dog's journey a privilege, an adventure and a true labor of love.

Acknowledgements

Fostering a puppy for possible assistance, training a therapy dog, rescuing a shelter dog or raising a well-behaved pet are not easy tasks. They are joint efforts among owners, families, friends, relatives, trainers and even strangers who lend assistance throughout these endeavors.

While I thank all of those people who have assisted with training and socialization, there are certain individuals who deserve special recognition for their efforts.

First and foremost, I must thank my wonderful husband, **Chuck Trojan**, for his continued support, enthusiasm and assistance while writing this book. Because of his love, encouragement, patience and countless proof reading, this story was written.

Many thanks to **Pam Osbourne** who not only served as an exceptional consultant in the preparation of the book but was also instrumental in the final printing process including the book's formatting. Her expertise contributed significantly toward the completion of the book. She is also a talented writer and extremely patient friend.

Kim Stephenson, of Paw Prints Pix Photography,

graciously granted permission and licensing use of the cover photos, Wall of Fame photo and Having a Ball photo. Her skill and expertise are evident in terms of the quality of images and cover designs. **Kim's** talent, generosity and patience are greatly appreciated.

Kathleen Deist, the Goddess of Grammar and Punctuation, served as one of the proof readers for the book. As a former English teacher, her expertise in the areas of punctuation and grammar proved extremely helpful toward its completion. Please don't

hold her accountable for my not using semicolons. She indicated their usage in some paragraphs, but I disregarded them and clarified my position in the disclaimer. Having **Kathleen** as a consultant for my books has been an incredible experience; having her as my friend is the greater gift.

Mary Krystinak, the Countess of Computers, assisted me with portions of this book. I'm so very grateful for her computer expertise, her availability and endless patience while working with me. I am especially fortunate to call her my friend.

Jan Jaeger of Charlotte, North Carolina, became a good friend years ago when we both raised siblings for an assistance organization. I thank her for sharing her pictures of Kelyn (Kessen's sister), Charlie, Carly, Sidney and Beppe for events in the book. While we live far apart and don't talk as often as I'd like,  we have a special bond, and that bond is one of friendship across the miles. Bless her heart!

Carol DeMaio, the Comma Queen and a valued friend of many years, served as one of my proof readers. Her productive insights provided invaluable assistance toward the completion of this book. **Carol** never once let her friendship with me stand in the way of constructive criticism. I truly appreciate her time, expertise and, above all, her enduring friendship.

Father Slawik Ignasik blessed each of the dogs before we took them to Puppy College. Knowing the dogs were beginning the next chapter in their lives with a special blessing from him made giving up the dogs a bit easier. **Father Ignasik** had a special love for each of the dogs, and his interaction with them demonstrated his  love. We are so very grateful for his blessings over the years.

255

 **Julia Havey** was kind enough to share her wonderful dog named **Linus** with our family. Sweet **Linus**, who specialized in the unique socialization of puppies, spent time with each of our dogs and worked his magic through his Three Step Action Plan. I am most grateful for their assistance.

Rachel Woodward, Joy Rittierodt and Nivin Wynn

The trainers at **Narnia Pet Behavior and Training Center** have provided exceptional guidance for each of the dogs we raised. These trainers shared their talents and expertise through instruction, lively demonstrations and individual attention during each of the classes.

For many years, **Panera Bread** has been a major advocate for assistance dogs in training. The staff consistently welcomed the dogs into their establishment. By doing that, they assisted in the dogs' journeys toward being silent guardians to the disabled. To acknowledge their efforts, they were the recipients of the **Prestigious Paw Award** from **Paws with a Cause. Turin, Kessen, Brightie, Marnie, Izzy, Tans**y and **Nixie** can't thank them enough for their efforts.

I do wish to thank those individuals who allowed me to use names and photographs of their dogs in this book:

The Saltarelli Family (Izzy), **Jan Jaeger** (Kelyn, Charlie, Carly, Sidney and Beppe), **Amie Harpe** (Benelli, and Naomi), **Pam and Rick Osbourne** (Rufus), **The Poturica Family** (Sammy), **Rochelle Byrd** (Deon a.k.a. Deonna), **Lisa Kruss** (Wall of Fame individual photos of Kessen, Turin and Brightie), **Julia Havey** (Linus), **Mike Weimer** (Harley), **Marie Castellano and Mary Nobbe** (Miller) the **Mahler Family** (Turin), **Felicia Montesarchi**o (Dawson), **Joan Lester** and the **Fehrenbach Family** (Bart) and **Linda** and **Grady Moorer** (Lulu and Milani).

Special thanks to the **assistance organizations** across the country that provide puppies for fostering and to the **puppy raisers** who share in the puppy's journey. Fostering a puppy for potential assistance is an experience that lingers in the heart and mind forever.

Finally, I sincerely thank all **assistance dogs** and **therapy dogs** for the work they do for others. On any given day, most of us can't even imagine how much they do to help others in need. Special treats for all of you

IN MEMORIAM

Beppe, Buddy, Carly, Dawson, Deon, Duffy, Echo,

Gretzky, Jasmine, Kaiser, Kessen, Kiya, Klaus,

Linus, Lulu, Max, Merlin, Miller, Naomie,

Rebound, Roscoe, Sammy, Shamus, Sidney,

Turin, Vanessa, Wynston, Yoshe, Zachary and

our dear Brightie

They gave us unconditional love
and
left paw prints on our hearts.

Forever in our hearts...

CPSIA information can be obtained
at www.ICGtesting.com
Printed in the USA
FSOW04n1536081017
39476FS